Dispute Resolution within Africa

Rashri Baboolal Frank
Editor

Dispute Resolution within Africa

A Journey Forward

Springer

Editor
Rashri Baboolal Frank
Procedural Law
University of Pretoria
Pretoria, South Africa

ISBN 978-3-031-76260-4 ISBN 978-3-031-76261-1 (eBook)
https://doi.org/10.1007/978-3-031-76261-1

This Springer imprint is published by the registered company Springer Nature Switzerland AG
The registered company address is: Gewerbestrasse 11, 6330 Cham, Switzerland

Preface

The main topic is alternative dispute resolution within specific African countries, and the journey of Africa becoming a global leader as the seat of dispute resolution, focusing on the mechanisms of mediation, arbitration, conciliation and negotiation. Through the Masters in Alternative Dispute Resolution emerged this collaborative opportunity to engage critically about topics discussed in class, intuitively chosen topics for exploration in mini dissertations and essays culminated into a very focused contribution to the African continent. In international commercial transactions, it is inviolable that disputes arise, and the commercial contracts provides for a med-arb clause, and parties go to private forums to resolve the dispute. Negotiation becomes a key tactic embedded into the mediation techniques and style adopted, to ensure success of proceedings. If mediation fails then arbitration is the last stage to determine the finality of the dispute, when an award is given after hearing evidence, this final award is not appealable. The journey of Africa being a global leader and encouraging partnerships with global institutions, practices and international trends is an ideal, and it is a journey that is necessary to overtake the European and American seats of dispute resolution.

The aim of the book is to provide a current manuscript for dispute resolution in Africa. Dispute Resolution is a current topic that is constantly evolving in sight of the fourth industrial resolution, yet there is not a current book debating current topical issues of contention, that required deeper reflection and novelty about this discussion relating to selected African countries. This book aims to deal with the current dispute resolution topics within an African context. The collaborators are also from the African region, which gives this book the cutting-edge research and relevancy for the African global contextual narrative.

The audience of the book is academics and scholars that study dispute resolution within the African continent. This area is still being developed as Africa uses the existence knowledge of resolving conflicts together with western methods as is evident from the urbanisation.

This book has been double blindly peer reviewed for quality assurance and to ensure scholarship relevance. The publisher has maintained ethical standards at all times.

Pretoria, South Africa Rashri Baboolal Frank

Competing Interests

There are no competing interests.

Ethics Approval No ethics approval was required as the research conducted was desktop research.

Contents

Contents

Chapter 1
Artificial Intelligence Readiness in Africa

R. Baboolal-Frank

1.1 Introduction

Africa has wealth of opportunity. There is abundance of natural resources, yet there is not enough for the greed of Man to disseminate. The world is moving forward in the fourth industrial revolution with technology taking the lead. With the advent of technology as the praecipe there has been adaptations to alternative dispute resolution more than could have been imagined 10 years ago. Online dispute resolution possesses a multitude of benefits in that it is convenience, no legal representation is required, even if a person is illiterate the processes will continue using Chatbots and machine generated artificial intelligence.[1] Audit firms have projected that the revue and growth that artificial intelligence (AI) can generate in different sectors such as health, agriculture, society, commerce exceeds in trillions of dollars.[2] This means that there is a multitude of wealth and enrichment to be gained when more funds are invested into building and expanding artificial intelligence within the African region.

[1] Sebayiga (2023), p. 1.

[2] Sebayiga (2023), pp. 1–8.

R. Baboolal-Frank (✉)
University of Pretoria, Department of Procedural Law, Faculty of Law, Pretoria, South Africa
e-mail: rashri.baboolal@up.ac.za

R. Baboolal Frank (ed.), *Dispute Resolution within Africa*,
https://doi.org/10.1007/978-3-031-76261-1_1

Table 1.1 Artificial intelligence readiness for Top 3 tier African countries

Country	Total score	Government pillar	Technology sector pillar	Data and infrastructure pillar
61. Mauritius	53.27	69.82	30.63	59.35
62. Egypt	52.69	68.19	40.11	49.77
77. South Africa	47.28	37.82	40.22	63.79

1.2 Artificial Intelligence Readiness

Oxford conducted a study of the readiness of African countries development of artificial intelligence and ranked South African as 77 which is below Egypt as 62 and Mauritius which is number 61 in the world.[3] The index score ranking composes of three categories namely government pillar, technology sector pillar and lastly data infrastructure pillar.

The table of scores (Table 1.1) are divided into government, technology sector and data infrastructure for the top three African countries for artificial readiness.[4] It is interesting to note that the government pillar is the weakest score, due to the political instability, as well as the lack of accountability and accounts of corruption since state capture reports in South Africa. The government lacks controls over the respective tiers within administration of government and it is seen in the scoring, when the factors are taken into account. On the contrary the strength in score was the data and infrastructure pillar, it is apparent that in the capital cities, that access to data, is of good supply and connection albeit the loadshedding connection interferes with the strength of the data and fibre connections, but it still works with back-up power supply such as generators, solar panels and inverters.

The three pillars composing the empirical data measuring the Artificial Intelligence is detailed to ensure the comprehensive readiness. The government requires a strategic vision for the development, regulation and detail to ethical risk comprising transparency, accountability and governance. The responsibility for government is to ensure that there is sufficient digital capacity which comprises of skills, practice, support and adapting to the advanced and innovative technologies.[5] The technology sector requires that there is a sufficient supply of innovation, entrepreneurial skills, research and development spending, human capital and educated and specialised people working on the improvement and enhancement of this sector.[6] In terms of the composition of Data and Infrastructure the artificial intelligence tools must be

[3]Oxford Insights(2023) https://oxfordinsights.com/wp-content/uploads/2023/12/2023-Government-AI-Readiness-Index-1.pdf [Accessed 30 November 2023].

[4]Oxford Insights (2023) https://oxfordinsights.com/wp-content/uploads/2023/12/2023-Government-AI-Readiness-Index-1.pdf at 49.

[5]Oxford Insights (2023), p. 5.

[6]Oxford Insights (2023), p. 5.

clinically perfect and needs to be representative of the demographic population and to fuel the tools and ensure service delivery to the respective citizens.[7]

It must be noted that one of the barriers to AI readiness is the notion of the digital divide between the North and Southern hemispheres. There is a disparity in the supply of data coupled with insecure infrastructure. There is also the predisposition to bias in the respective AI tools in addition there are language barriers if there is AI that is not developed within the respective national languages for the country, which may impose challenges and drawbacks for the development of AI.[8]

The countries that are the lower income, but still stand in good stead with the respective STEM research and engineering graduates and general tertiary education quality are China, India, Russia and Malaysia as their research papers, both India and China, are in the top three relating to AI research. It is notable that Russia, China and India are still leaders in terms of the research and development component, that is well orchestrated and communicated to global platforms, despite other drawbacks and setbacks as developing countries.

With the advent of AI it becomes a necessary measure to improve data regulation as well as to provide for regulation for AI, as AI has the potential to generate a lot of revenue as has been seen with the AI health care technology for mothers. However, the digital divide still exists with Africa, food insecurity, poverty, disease and illness, illiteracy, unemployment, discrimination and religious wars and land disputes to mention a few.[9] There are many aspects that still requires redress and improvement to fully be equipped with AI and to the future forward thinking.

1.3 Regulation of AI

There are guidelines in the use of AI, emphasis on the responsible use of machine generated technology.[10] Navigating through regulations still leave many unanswered questions, such as AI assist for the creation of patent laws, is not recognised by entities that are not capable of being represented by a human.[11] Polycentric governance framework is very broadly term used to informally govern AI, in a multi-disciplinary approach that is community centric.[12] The formulation of Artificial Intelligence finds it roots embedded within ancient civilisations.[13] It is evident, in constructing a term of definition for AI is rather limiting, as it is so broad and an encapsulation of knowledge as well as self-learning processes. It is important to

[7] Oxford Insights (2023), p. 5.

[8] Oxford Insights (2023), pp. 5–7.

[9] Jaldi (2023), pp. 1–25.

[10] OECD Principles of 2019. AU guidelines on the use of AI.

[11] Furnival (2022), p. 24.

[12] Shackelford and Dockery (2020), p. 283.

[13] Shackelford and Dockery (2020), p. 284.

navigate the challenges to AI to provide guidance how to navigate to solutions and prevent the same barriers.[14] Cyber safety is of paramount importance interlinked to safety engineering and to ensure physical safety of the users utilising the artificial intelligence.[15] The consequences of these challenges is of course damages that arise, invariably there is be ethical, legal and governance repercussions.[16] The economic projections was that automation would replace people but invariably create more jobs, which would mean that people would still have a place, of work, however the future of employment will be different to the way we have been accustomed to it, with the AI parameters, and would require labour law regulations and amendments.[17] Social and cultural implications, as a human society feel undermined[18] when replaced by artificial intelligence, so to create the harmony and synergy between the two role players requires a careful balance and consideration of emotions, appreciation and value. Legal and ethical implications are important in the navigation of transferral of human qualities to artificial intelligence, and also allowing for understanding processes through emotions, trustworthiness as these aspects mimic humans in machine generated intelligence, which has ethical and human consequences for the global world, and we have to be careful how we navigate forward with the hope of robotic futures in our present workplaces.

1.4 ADR and AI

There have been numerous progressions of reporting using Artificial Intelligence to input algorithms to be an AI ADR practitioner for simplistic matters, that are prompted through each step, such as consumer disputes, when the resolution is reached the outcomes, are either, return and refund, or exchange or given a credit note to spend for the future consumer purchases. AI generated arbitrators inputting the intelligence and thinking of real lawyers is an ethical conundrum, as a machine is not a person with ethical values, it can be inputted, but is still morally reprehensible, for example if a mistake is committed who takes accountability, is it the manager of the AI or the machine, is it even possible. It seems for now, that a machine can take accountability when programmed to do so, but is still problematic for peace of mind for hassle free disputes. Using AI programmes to resolve construction disputes with the AI ADR practitioner that mediates the dispute for the most part to settlement. It is apparent that these different contexts operate within the bounds of limitation, the way we understand AI to work, still under suspicion and mistrust. Within the lessons

[14] Shackelford and Dockery (2020), p. 296.

[15] Shackelford and Dockery (2020), p. 296.

[16] Shackelford and Dockery (2020), p. 296.

[17] Shackelford and Dockery (2020), p. 297.

[18] Shackelford and Dockery (2020), p. 298.

of polycentric governance is conflict resolution mechanisms,[19] this is important, as with daily sectors there is conflict and mechanisms are important to navigate to solutions and resolution of disputes between parties involved or affected by artificial intelligence that could cause possible damage, short or future term. When we look towards unpacking the terms of artificial intelligence, there are qualities that it imbibes such as the replication of human behaviour that has been inputted through algorithms and using big data storage.[20]

1.5 AI Principles

The Organisation for Economic Co-operation and Development published ten principles that were divided into five value based principles and the remainder recommendations for policy makers. The value based principles are "inclusive growth, sustainable development and well-being." This principle aligns to the nourishment that AI should serve and uphold the sustainable development goals in the growth and development of people and nations. "Human-centred values and fairness" it is noteworthy that AI can be more intelligent that a human, and then it is important that the machine be benchmarked on a human level qualities since it exceeds human capabilities and intelligence, it is important that humans are judged, measured and equated to their own markers of fairness. Although may seem contrived, AI to malfunction or cause malware has possible devastating consequences. "Transparency and explainability" there needs to be clear guidelines in the use and application of AI tools and programmes, it should not be hidden. Transparency ensures openness and honesty. This aspect interlinks to the accountability principle. The last value based principle is "robustness, security and safety" in a context of global hacking, stealing cryptocurrency, the internet is used to commit various crimes and fraud. AI is more sophisticated technology able to control big data, this is a serious responsibility, on both the users and creators hence security and safety is of paramount importance for everyone. These security measure needs to be apt, robust, clinical and necessary. The recommendations for policy makers are practical and pragmatic. "Investing in AI R&D" the only way to build, refine and improve systems is to continuously invest in the research and development initiatives, to progress forward. "Fostering a digital ecosystem for AI" ensuring that there is a digital community of AI sharing resources and to assist each other in navigating through barriers and challenges, similarly to the African proverb that "you go far when you go together." "Providing an enabling policy environment for AI" this is the careful, meticulous planning that needs to occur, to prepare for present, current and future eventualities, and prepare the essential policies, that will be amended as time passes, as do all pieces of policy. "Building human capacity and preparing for labour market

[19] Shackelford and Dockery (2020), p. 333.

[20] Chen (2019–2020), p. 43.

transitions" this is invariable, as AI replaces human capital, more employment is created required for human capital to full those posts, there would need to be labour regulations, regulating the workplace and AI. "International co-operation for trustworthy" We live in a global community and need to cooperate with each other on the basis of trust, create AI that has integrity and honesty to build and foster global economies for scale. For Australia AI Ethics Principle, the only aspect not overlapping was "Contestability" to provide an opportunity challenge the consequences or outcomes of AI, which ensures adequate reporting and feedback from the public. The African Union are focusing on strengthening data legislation and regulation, using current systems and human capital for building and harmonising knowledge to address the AI challenges and research and development.

1.6 Recommendations

Artificial intelligence is growing and expanding at an alarming rate. From self-automated cars, to domestic robots to robotic assist during surgical procedures, there have been a wide array of developments. Using artificial intelligence is indeed more accurate and in some instances more superior and advanced than the human eye. However, with all the positivity of AI, there is of course the nature eventuality of disputes that will arise. There will be disputes that arise from the dissemination of information from AI, there will be disputes from the use of AI for example. There will also be ADR facilities created using machine learning and hence will be self-automated, to ensure that as many simplistic disputes are resolved in these stepped processes. Partner with current STEM institutes to share resources and knowledge and invest in the future research. The more research undertaken the more knowledge gained which will empower to move forward into the future.

1.7 Conclusion

South Africa can improve the readiness score with more government focus on eradicating corruption, government being accountable and transparent. Government investing in STEM research, encouraging female graduates, creating opportunities through bursary and full funding opportunities. More investment into the energy crisis in South Africa, amending legislation to provide for supply of electricity to be opened and not monopolised to one provide that is on crutches as the liquidity of Eskom is in crisis. The machinery is on the brink of breakdown, and South Africa is a step away from complete black out, which would have devastating and crippling consequences for the country that is not easily reversed if at all. The more we partner national and internationally regarding AI tools, research, development, the more promise and opportunity lies ahead as a glimmer of hope.

References

Chen ML (2019–2020) Impact of artificial intelligence on the professional responsibilities of lawyers. Sing Law Rev 37:43

Furnival T (2022) The case for AI Inventorship flounders. Manag Intellect Prop 294:22

Jaldi A (2023) Artificial intelligence revolution in Africa: economic opportunities and legal challenges. Policy Center for the New South, p. 1–25

OECD Principles of 2019. AU guidelines on the use of AI

Oxford Insights (2023). https://oxfordinsights.com/wp-content/uploads/2023/12/2023-Government-AI-Readiness-Index-1.pdf

Sebayiga V (2023)Evaluating the role of technology powered Alternative Dispute Resolution (ADR) in a Post Pandemic Africa. https://www.researchgate.net/profile/Vianney-Sebayiga/publication/367555009_Evaluating_the_Role_of_Technology-Powered_Alternative_Dispute_Resolution_ADR_in_a_Post-Pandemic_Africa/links/63ea77ddeab072152f4356ee/Evaluating-the-Role-of-Technology-Powered-Alternative-Dispute-Resolution-ADR-in-a-Post-Pandemic-Africa.pdf

Shackelford SJ, Dockery R (2020) Governing AI. Cornell J Law Public Policy 2:279

Professor Rashri Baboolal-Frank joined the Department of Procedural Law in the Faculty of Law at the University of Pretoria as a lecturer in February 2014. Prior to joining the University she practised as an attorney in Cape Town, Western Cape. She practised commercial litigation, criminal law, general litigation and resolution of property disputes. Subsequently to gaining experience as an attorney, she sought to become an advocate. She removed herself as a practising attorney and enrolled as an advocate after completing the necessary pupillage training and required exams. Prof. Baboolal-Frank was promoted to Senior Lecturer in February 2019. Prof. Baboolal-Frank was promoted to Associate Professor in January 2023.

She completed her LLB at the University of KwaZulu Natal. She obtained her Master's degree in Commercial Law (LLM) from the University of Cape Town. She completed her LLD from the University of Pretoria entitled "A Critical Analysis of Tribunals in South Africa to create a harmonised tribunal system". She completed the AFSA postgraduate certificate course in Alternative Dispute Resolution in conjunction with the University of Pretoria *cum laude*. She holds her Master's in Business Administration (MBA) from the University of South Wales in the United Kingdom. Prof. Baboolal-Frank is a leader in her field, as she is a C3 rated scholar by the National Research Foundation due to the plethora of quality scholarship published nationally and internationally. She also holds her BSC (Biomedical) with distinction from the University of South Africa. She has successfully won numerous cases as the leading counsel for litigious cases. She is cited by her peers in academic work. She has been contacted by the media to give her legal opinion. She is often invited as a book reviewer for books that are published in her field and are internationally recognised. She is a peer reviewer for more than ten international and national journals that are recognised, accredited and indexed. She is a registered ADR practitioner on the Commercial and Generalist Panel for Arbitration Foundation of Southern Africa. She is a member of the Chartered Institute of Arbitrators, she is a member of the Asian Institute of Alternative Dispute Resolution, and an Associate Member of the Singapore Institute of Arbitrators.

Chapter 2
An Overview of Alternative Dispute Resolution in Africa

K. Mgwenyana

"In the middle of difficult times lies opportunity"–Albert Einstein

2.1 Introduction

Disputes are a natural consequence of conflict. They culminate into serious matters when it is clear that relations have broken down.[1] However, in as much as conflicts may be inevitable, the same does not necessarily apply to disputes.[2] We should do our best to "handle conflicts and prevent disputes."[152] The type of approach taken to resolve a conflict is largely dependent on what caused the disparity.[3] There are several options available to resolve a matter.[4] Parties may ignore the dispute, attempt to discuss among themselves, or even obtain the help of an outsider, an independent third party, to settle the matter.[5]

2.2 Defining Concepts

The following concepts are defined below.

This chapter is based on the LLM mini dissertation of the author K Mwenyana that is available on the UP repository website.

[1] Ntuli (2018), p. 37.

[2] Nelson (2000), p. 3.

[3] Chowdhury (2016), p. 15.

[4] Greco (2010), pp. 656–657.

[5] Ntuli (2018), para 4.

K. Mgwenyana (✉)
University of Pretoria, Pretoria, South Africa

R. Baboolal Frank (ed.), *Dispute Resolution within Africa*,
https://doi.org/10.1007/978-3-031-76261-1_2

2.2.1 Conciliation

The conciliation process is a three-part dispute resolution process that progresses to mediation and ends in arbitration. It is voluntary and requires a positive and participatory approach[6] from both parties to reach a mutual outcome.[7] The person who performs this arduous task of bringing the parties together should first understand human behaviour[158] and preferably have the requisite legal training and possess other competencies that will allow them to navigate this task. A good level head and a high degree of emotional intelligence will stand him or her in good stead.[159] This fluid process offers an opportunity for the parties to put forward their version of events[8] and for the conciliator to delve into the issues raised in an open, non-prejudicial manner,[9] it provides an inquisitorial opportunity. It is expected of the conciliator to apply his mind to the whole body of facts and find a rational outcome to the dispute, bearing in mind the unique set of facts they are dealing with.[10] Having this awareness assists him to navigate the type of dispute better, as some are more complex than others due to the emotions invested in the matter and the intricacy of the possible outcome.[11] The process of conciliation has always best been used in the employment sphere of resolving employment disputes. Its found success in the manner the bargaining structures and units are designed to foster sound labour relations and is always advisable for the disputant parties to attend to employment matters in a conciliatory mode.[12]

2.2.2 Mediation

Mediation is a process that requires those in conflict to attend and arrive at the mediation with some level or form of compromise.[13] Simply put, you cannot mediate without the presence of conflict; this is the rational theory of mediation.[14] The power of the process is found in the goal-setting focus and nature.[15] The outlook of resolve by the disputants is largely assisted by the physical presence of a third party who will resolve the conflict. The success of the mediation depends on this

---

[6] Christensen (2014), p. 584.

[7] Wenying (2005), p. 959.

[8] Smith (1978), p. 206.

[9] Blignaut (2018), p. 26.

[10] Kopec and Titelbaum (2016), p. 189.

[11] Howard and Graham (1982), p. 90.

[12] Teper (1949), p. 563.

[13] Marcello (2010), p. 349. Nor does conciliation mean that the conflicts have been neutralized, as if all positions were equivalent.

[14] Terris and Maoz (2005), p. 565.

[15] Wanis-St (2000), p. 345.

skillset.[16] The third party depends wholly on the genuineness of participation and ultimately their agreement on implementing the outcome. The mediator is often required to dig a little deeper within themself to bring parties to their desired outcome.[17] Although the mediation process is flexible, resolving it depends on the nature of the conflict, the willingness of the parties to actually reach consensus, and the experience or skillset of the mediator to steer the process towards such an end.[18] Some might argue there is much emphasis placed on even the premediation phase, which may prove critical to resolving the conflict, as it aids with planning the session and its preparation.[19]

The mediator always needs to be aware of his contributions in resolving the matter.[20] This means there are implicit, tacit behavioural concessions attributable to them only, which could hamper the process if left unchecked.[21] The mediator contributes to the process in thought or intention, which both influence the environment, the physical space, the emotion of the parties, and the psychology of others.[22] Hyman elucidates the importance of deliberating on the moral foundations of the mediation process because underlying the process is the need for a sense of fairness, which is integral for good outcomes.[23]

2.2.3 *Arbitration*

The arbitration process is the final leg of the three-stage dispute resolution process, with a more formal legalistic approach than its two predecessors. The adjudicator needs to display the rational thought of applying the law to the facts before reaching a binding conclusion.[24] This requires precision and experience because the arbitrator does not want to be too legalistic or technical without allowing for a measure of flexibility, his acumen must be impeccable.[25] The theory behind the concept is premised on a winner and a loser outcome.[26] Unfortunately, the outcome can only favour one party, but the arbitrator should always be conscious of providing a balanced reasoned basis for his outcome.[27]

---

[16] Ntuli (2018), p. 57.

[17] Verbeek (2012), pp. 391–395.

[18] Schmitz (2001), pp. 190–194.

[19] Kermez (2010), p. 1.

[20] Jacobs and Aakhus (2002), p. 177.

[21] Bemmels (1991), pp. 548–551.

[22] Noll (2007), p. 37.

[23] Hyman (2015), p. 960.

[24] Reif (2007), p. 21

[25] Turner (2010), p. 21.

[26] Revesz (2014), p. 21.

[27] Revesz (2014), pp. 21–38.

The arbitration award is most influenced not only by the arbitrator's own psychology, legal training and experience, but the actual legal system from which they operate. When dealing with international arbitrations, aspects such as the seat of arbitration become of paramount importance because the national court gets to deal with enforceability. The arbitral award may have several legal implications for the enforceability of the award. Paulsson describes this as the parties wanting to be permitted to decide on the flexibility of the process but relying upon the legal protection of the State.[28]

2.3 Defining These Concepts to the African Context

International mediators should consider their mandate of mediation when dealing with matters since it provides explicit instructions concerning the nature of the assignment.[29] The mandate is given by either or both of the disputants, the instructing authority, which could be the tribunal from either parties home State consisting of a non-profit Organisation issuing the instruction.[30]

The flaw in the arbitral system, which the African continent must take cognisance of, is the lack of precedent. This means that arbitrators are not bound to take to the decisions already made by their peers, how judicial officers are. Perhaps one need not worry too much about that aspect. Comella refers to Fiss in her article, explaining that the courts have enough of that to deal with, and the arbitrators have the flexibility to be creative and original in their jurisprudence.[31] Like many other courts, African courts tend to follow a pro-arbitration and anti-litigation policy, where both approaches are mutually reinforcing.[32]

2.3.1 Schematic Overview of ADR in Africa

ADR practices are implemented in all 54 African countries, even though some have implemented more than others.[33]

The continent's legal landscape comprises a kaleidoscope of different laws, making it complex. Due to its diversity, Africa sees 6000 languages spoken on its continent. The culture infuses into the legal regimes, and the history of colonialism forms the basis of the common law, combined civil law with influences from Europe.

---

[28] Paulsson (2010), p. 2.

[29] Duursma (2014), p. 81.

[30] Duursma (2014), p. 96.

[31] Comella (2014), p. 13.

[32] Bookman (2019), p. 1122.

[33] Herbert Smith Freehills (2016), p. 5.

More importantly, are the religious influences of indigenous African people as their customary law is at the centre and also the Arabic and Islamic laws.[34] Successful implementation of ADR processes depends largely on the legal systems in place when the award is enforced. Generally, Africa has taken well to implementing ADR processes and have adapted their legal systems by enacting legislation in line with the international standards, allowing Africa to be considered as a partner in the peace-seeking efforts of sound dispute resolution, knowing that the investor can build confidence in its matters being handled with the requisite legal certainty.

2.4 Conclusion

The priority African governments place on the conciliatory processes, and their incorporation into the legislation is of paramount importance, as they greatly impact the success of such ADR processes. Governments that have recognised the value of the conciliations processes have yielded the necessary results. Once the State is a party to the dispute, it generally requires the court to order it to pay, because of public funds being at play, but when the State enters conciliation processes with openness and transparency and does not hide behind its immunity and red bureaucratic tape, it can reap the rewards of the process. States which also recognise the value which conciliatory processes bring to the employment environment, through the collective bargaining structures, profit. The proper working of the latter mechanisms foster sound labour relations between the employer and employee, resulting in a productive working class, which benefits the economy.

Mediation processes are also not far from the heritage of the African people and reflective of the history and roots of how the indigenous people negotiated to reach a compromise. Trust was and still is at the centre of the processes relied upon for the success of the mediation. Mediation as a form of ADR practice will always resonate with the African people because of its foundational core values of *'ubuntu'* and restorative social justice upon which it is premised. Overall, with international dispute settlement, the conciliation and arbitration processes are seen as more structured because of the ability of the third party to delve deep into the issues to extract the essence of the dispute and resolve it amicably, this approach better suits its parties. Both processes require the parties to provide a proper account of the facts for proper investigation into the resolve to take place. In conclusion, Africa confronts similar challenges faced by other countries where there are huge delays in the finalisation of cases. Mediation can assist with the challenge of the backlogs. Court annexed mediation is a practical and effective means of decreasing the backlogs and is welcomed in most African countries. The State's firm commitment to enforce this route through enacted legislation has proven successful in Nigeria, Ghana and SA, but to mention a few. ADR in Africa should be embraced in its

[34] Herbert Smith Freehills (2016), p. 6.

court's structures first before it can be fully effective in the commercial industry because enforceability of awards always comes back to the courts for implementation.

2.5 Recommendation

Africa should recognise the importance of the investor to its economy and its role in maintaining sound business relations for the growth of the African economy. Nevertheless, Africa cannot compromise on principles of equality to eliminate undue perception created of bias towards the investor.[35] The practical implementation of the ADR into the justice system will allow Africa to reap further rewards in terms of quick resolution of less complex matters and a decreased court roll. Therefore, it is recommended that the African continent look at its legislation and how it prioritises ADR into the formal court system and laws of the country to allow for legal certainty for both investors and citizens.

2.6 A Critique of ADR Institutions in Africa

2.6.1 Introduction

This chapter offers a critique of ADR institutions in Africa. It looks to the various influences of ADR in Africa by turning to the main arbitral seats and seeks to understand how the OHADA agreement impacts member and non-member States. In delving into the institutions, one must be mindful of the dawn of the Fourth Industrial Revolution (4IR) and its impact on ADR processes in the African continent and globally. The transformation of ADR in Africa should also be adaptive to Online Dispute Resolution (ODR), which is the future of ADR.

2.6.2 Influences of ADR in Africa

Disputes in Africa are solved by imploring ADR methods, particularly in a commercial settlement, where mediation processes are preferred. The rise of foreign investment into Africa due to its ever-growing and expanding economies[36] has increased in dispute matters. In establishing the main arbitral centres in Africa, the

[35] Mojtaba and Afshin (2018), p. 68.

[36] Herbert Smith Freehills (2016), p. 5.

continent has displayed its capability to manage and resolve investor conflict through these institutions.

The bi-and multilateral treaties entered into with African member States ensure peaceful enforcement and resolve disputes on the continent. The OHADA, which stands for the Organisation for the Harmonisation of Business Law in Africa, greatly assists in this respect. It is a significant multilateral treaty because it was contracted into by 17 African countries in 1993.[37] However, SA is not a party to such. The main African arbitral centres in Africa include SA, Mauritius, Egypt, Nigeria and, for arbitration under the OHADA Uniform Act, Côte d'Ivoire.[38] Comparative law has a vital role in developing and evaluating cross-border dispute resolution, hence the need to distinguish party members to the OHADA.

The OHADA member countries have made great strides for the African continent, where Mauritius has proven its success through the launch of its international centre and cemented this in its close working relations with the Londonbased international arbitration institution, the LCIA (LCIA-MIAC).[39] Egypt has adopted a modern arbitration law based on the UNCITRAL model law, its Cairo Regional Centre for international commercial arbitration amended its rules in 2011 to conform with the 2010 UNCITRAL arbitration rules.[40] The Ivory Coast has established the Common Court of Justice and Arbitration (CCJA), this is both a permanent arbitration institution and Supreme court of arbitration for.

OHADA member States.[41] Nigeria has its regional centre, ICA Lagos, and Maritime Arbitrators Association of Nigeria (MANN); Lagos Court of Arbitration ranked as the highest African arbitration institution; the International Centre for Arbitration and Mediation, Abuja (ICAMA); and the Lagos Chamber of Commerce International Arbitration Centre and Janada International Centre of Arbitration and mediation, Abuja.[42] SA, too, proves itself capable of holding an international arbitral centre as it has main national arbitration institutions, albeit a non-OHADA member, and has established the Arbitration Foundation of Southern Africa (AFSA), and the Association of Arbitrators whose rules are based on the 2010 UNCITRAL Arbitration Rules prove competent.[195] SAs enactment of the International Arbitration Act in 2017 demonstrates its capability to be a preferred arbitral centre.[43] Further, the China Africa Joint Arbitration centre, which AFSA launched, is dedicated to resolving commercial disputes between Chinese and African parties. SA is a member of BRICS, this makes sense to foster such relations for bettering its economy.[44] The establishment of arbitral courts in Africa allows for the binding decisions from

[37] Herbert Smith Freehills (2016), p. 9.

[38] Herbert Smith Freehills (2016), p. 9.

[39] Herbert Smith Freehills (2016), p. 9.

[40] Herbert Smith Freehills (2016), para 2.

[41] Herbert Smith Freehills (2016), para 2.

[42] Browning (2017), p. 22.[195]; Herbert Smith Freehills (2016), p. 268.

[43] Browning (2017), p. 23.

[44] Herbert Smith Freehills (2016), p. 5.

domestic courts, which are legally enforceable on both members and "non-consenting third parties."[45] These bold developments on the African continent display its tenacity and progressive nature to leading and being at the fore of ADR implementation. The main arbitral seats on the continent offer investor confidence and protection, which boosts the economy of the continent, to the "classical investors," which are the US, Great Britain, Canada and France.[46]

2.6.3 *Transformation of ADR in Africa*

The African continent must be mindful of the need to transform its ADR approaches to keep up with the technological advances and developments in the world, especially to accommodate ODR, which is the future of ADR.[47] Online disputes arise when commercial transactions increase, and these transactions are normally referred to as e-commerce disputes (e-disputes).[48] The disputes are related to fraud, differences in culture, language barriers and problems in payment and delivery of goods.[49] The traditional ADR characteristics[50] are being overhauled,[51] due to the changes and development brought about by technology, because of the advent of the 4IR. The recent COVID-19 world pandemic has just further demonstrated the need to limit physical contact and has placed heavy reliance on the use of technology because of the compulsory social distance requirement. Artificial intelligence (AI) has more so than ODR stamped its place as the future because of its use of robotics in the substation of the human element. ADRs transformation journey embraces AI to enhance its efficiency of processes.[52] Currently, however, it would seem the aim is not to remove the mediator and substitute with a robot but to direct the parties on a better course of action through advising them on how to arrive at an amicable resolution.[53] To this end, there is an emergence of interactive online platforms, which automate even negotiations.[54] Foreign institutions which have displayed much progress in implementing ODR are the International Chamber of Commerce, American Arbitration Association (AAA) and World Intellectual Property Organi-

[45] Bookman (2021), p. 165.
[46] Herbert Smith Freehills (2016), p. 5.
[47] Ononogbu (2015), p. 77.
[48] Fahimeh et al. (2019), pp. 357–392.
[49] Fahimeh et al. (2019), p. 359.
[50] Blankley et al. (2010), p. 30.
[51] Parker and Hagin (1993), p. 1910.
[52] Peruginell (2002).
[53] Peruginell (2002).
[54] Mell and Gratch (2016).

sation.[55] It is advisable for the African continent to learn from this and implemented alongside its counterparts.

2.6.4 Online Dispute Resolution in Africa

ODR involves the use of computer-generated formulae to aid in resolving the dispute, where at times the presence of the third party is not required, this form of ODR is already successfully implemented by E-Bay.[56] The success of ODR in E-Bay is attributed to its resolve of over 35 million disputes successfully using ODR.[57] Technology is needed for almost every aspect of our daily living it has become an integral part of human existence, this can no longer be ignored, everything is now online.[58] Due to this rise in online activity, increased electronic disputes need to be resolved.[59] EBay has been the pioneer in this respect by showing how possible it is to settle a matter from ending online without being physically present.[60]

Africa has done well to embrace the technological changes the world faces in implementing ODR and bridging the 'digital justice gap'.[61] In as much as E-Bay has been at it since 1999, Kenya developed something, which showed its capability to advance its country by using technology, it introduced MPESA in 2007. This system allowed for the electronic payment similar to the E-Bay transactions, which allowed for optimal implementation and integration of ODR in its e-commerce.[62]

The benefits of ODR are that it is a secure manner of interaction, where confidentiality is regarded essential, the costs are convenient, and its accessible in an easy manner. The issue of convenience may prove to be the only drawback where the infrastructure is lacking but once in place its benefits far outweigh its disadvantages.[63] ODR can be seen implemented in many African States, but the infrastructure is a hindrance because of the economic climate in certain countries. At least, Nigeria and SA have proven themselves ready and capable of implementing ODR immediately, which is beneficial because accessing justice in this way is vital.[64] There have been proposals made to develop a framework for small businesses to assist in solving their disputes, referred to as INCADI.[65] This ODR platform maximises the SMEs

[55] Yuksel (2007), p. 84.

[56] Ononogbu (2015), p. 78.

[57] Ononogbu (2015), p. 78.

[58] Ononogbu (2015), para 1.

[59] Abedi et al. (2019), p. 358.

[60] Gonzalez (2003), p. 5.

[61] Porteous (2018), pp. 61–62.

[62] Ononogbu (2015), p. 79.

[63] Ononogbu (2015), p. 80.

[64] Roberge and Fraser (2019), p. 1.

[65] Roberge and Fraser (2019), p. 15.

interests (IN) and build on their capacity (CA) in the prevention and resolution of disputes (DI).[66] Africa may consider this model alongside the EU E-commerce Directive, and 2002 Regulations intended to safeguard citizens undertaking e-commerce; however, a limited number of African countries have followed suit.[67]

2.6.5 Conclusion

The online arbitrations and the traditional arbitrations display the same characteristics.[68] The only difference is the conclusion of proceedings through technology, be it video conferencing, skype, google meets, group chats or email. The traditional arbitration process is similar to civil trial hearings[69] where a parallel can be drawn between the two.[70] The move from face-to-face hearings to virtual hearings expands the innovation ofADR processes, which also requires the parties to adapt. ODR is the future of ADR and allows for a measure of flexibility and convenience but still has its challenges. These challenges are found in the enforcement of the award; the inability to reach consensus on interpreting the agreement, the lack of universally accepted ODR rules, and the laconic written feedback. Developing a uniform set of rules will have its challenges. Africa must be aware that the latter is not an all-encompassing solution with interpretation by different arbitrators. ODR must be embraced in Africa's transformation journey of ADRs but awareness of its flaws is important to circumvent whatever challenges may arise.

2.6.6 Recommendations

ODR is technology dependent. Africa thus has an obligation to ensure proper access to justice using technology. Albeit expensive, there is a further need to capacitate a diverse population on how to use the technology relied upon. Africa is already dealing with a host of real challenges, such as poverty, inequality and illiteracy. However, the right to access justice is equally important. The advent of 4IR has pressured governments to capacitate the older generations who are more reluctant to adapt to changing times and implement ODR platforms. Africa should put plans to utilise its resources efficiently to enable its people to have the necessary technological tools.

---

[66] Roberge and Fraser (2019), p. 17.

[67] Ononogbu (2015), p. 82.

[68] Parker and Hagin (1993), p. 1910.

[69] Deutsch (1990), p. 517–550.

[70] Harvey (1998), pp. 546–547.

International arbitrations concluded by African member States should consider aspects such as the enforceability of the agreement based on the selected seat of arbitration. The latter must be determined before finalising the ecommerce transaction. It is trite that the party autonomy is further reinforced in both the New York and European Conventions because they recognise that the enforcement of the award may be refused if the procedure was not in accordance with what was agreed to by the parties. Where the parties did not select online arbitration but find themselves faced with it,[71] the prevailing intention of the national and international legislation is important to be sought, and the decision of the tribunal may be accepted as final in the interests of proceeding with the matter. African tribunal must remain cognizant of this important aspect, as this is where the national legislation is important to be aligned with international legislative developments. The tribunal must always ensure parties are treated in the spirit of equitable principles.

2.7 Nexus Between ADR in Africa and Customary Practices

2.7.1 Introduction

This chapter deals with the nexus between ADR in Africa and customary practices. It analyses the modern approaches to ADR in Africa and seeks to demonstrate how Africa is adapting ADR to align it to its indigenous heritage. It illustrates the influences and access to justice in Africa by evaluating ADR in Africa and the role of Africa in International dispute resolution. Emphasis is also placed on the role played by African Elders in conflict resolution.

2.7.2 Assessing ADR in Africa

Africa embraced the use of ADR in its inherited post-colonialist legal system[72] to resolve those less serious disputes, has increased the public's confidence and perception of justice.[73] African countries are overwhelmed with backlogged cases, where litigation costs[74] are too expensive and unaffordable to the majority who are impoverished. According to Price, ADR, adoptive in form, was first developed in North America and grew to Europe and then Africa.[75] The adoptive form of ADR emanating from western culture had a major fallout in Africa because of its stark

[71] Waincymer (2020), p. 3.
[72] Ntuli (2018), p. 39.
[73] Price (2018), p. 2.
[74] Nwazi (2017), p. 27.
[75] Price (2018), p. 397.

contrast with African customary practices and incompatibility with indigenous customary practices.[76] Modern ADR in Africa needs to integrate traditional forms of dispute resolution, as Ghana did.[77] Ghana adapted ADR and successfully implemented certain African modifications, to ensure its best suited for the African context. These adaptations were underpinned by communal values and social cohesion, allowing Ghana to be viewed as the lead African country when implementing ADR.[78]

2.7.3 Modern Approaches to ADR in Africa

The modern ADR practices, which inherently depicts the traditional values of reconciliation and forgiveness, are most definitely not new concepts to Africa. These values have roots that date as far back as to the ancient African tribes of the Yoruba Nigerian and Kenyan people.[79] Similarly, in today's age, modern ADR practices have been incorporated into commercial transactions conducted on African territory to accommodate the world economy's globalisation and reduce the high litigation costs.[80] Modern ADR in Africa provides the continent with an opportunity to assess its traditional customary practices and see its integration into its modern-day application of ADR processes to improve conflict resolution for Africans based on their heritage and communal values.

2.7.4 ADR and Its Access to Justice in Africa

Conflict is sparked by diversity and the inability to synergise those divergent beliefs and views based on beliefs, values or personal interests.[81]Through proposals made by Prof Sander, the American literature hoped to go back to using some of the informal ways of resolving disputes used in ancient times.[82] He suggested the modern judicial system utilise "multi-door court house" which allows for a one-stop dispute resolution centre.[83] The proposal was forward thinking and resulted in successful pilot projects within the US[84] that also inspired many countries to

[76] Ordor and Aiyedun (2016), p. 158.
[77] Price (2018), p. 410.
[78] Price (2018), p. 396.
[79] Price (2018), p. 400.
[80] Price (2018), p. 401.
[81] Olufemi et al. (2019), p. 7.
[82] Olufemi et al. (2019), p. 7.
[83] Olufemi et al. (2019), p. 10.
[84] Jacobs and Aakhus (2002), p. 177.

follow. SA has demonstrated its following being implemented in the court annexed mediation. The African continent can follow this approach taken by SA, especially considering the advantages. African countries are incorporating ADR into their process to improve access to justice.[85] Ghana adapted ADR in its court system by allocating an increased number of mediators in its circuit courts to deal with cases, increasing its settlement rate.[86] Uganda followed by making mediation compulsory and ensuring the payment of the mediators and maintenance of the system through an established judiciary fund.[87] Nigeria also looked at introducing ADR for minor offences in the courts, and introduced ADR at schools where the school peer mediation pilot projects resulted in decreased violence and increased school attendance.[88] These efforts by the African countries show the adaptation of ADR to provide access to justice to their communities.

2.7.5 Evaluating ADR in Africa in International Dispute Resolution

Africa is using ADR to instill peaceful resolution of its disputes to foster innovation and lead to harmonisation.[89] The pilot project was initiated in Nigeria, where ADR is brought to the level of youth at school to decrease teenage violence and increase school attendance.[90] The introduction of this is a commendable way of using ADR, because its aim is to reduce an overcrowded and overworked juvenile system in the criminal justice system. Africa has joined the PCA by ensuring 22 of its States are members, where the cumulative number is 115. The PCA was established in 1899 with a Convention for the Pacific Settlement of International disputes.[91] African countries have submitted themselves to the jurisdiction of the court, and have seen 133 arbitrations involving African parties (which happen to be the State, private individuals and State owned companies) being concluded, all this from the period 1996 to 2014.[92] The PCA deals with various types of disputes involving African countries, which involve investor-State disputes, maritime disputes, boundary disputes and even political conflict.[93] There has been a clear rise in the number of referrals from 2000, where 80% of matters are taken to the PCA for adjudication.[94]

[85] Cohen and Alberstein (2019), p. 4.

[86] Price (2018), p. 410.

[87] Price (2018), p. 410.

[88] Price (2018), p. 416.

[89] Price (2018), p. 416.

[90] Price (2018), p. 416.

[91] Bosman 2014), p. 309.

[92] Bosman (2014), p. 311.

[93] Bosman (2014), p. 313.

[94] Bosman (2014), p. 313.

The work of the PCA where it involves cross-border conflict is invaluable because of its peace-seeking aim.[95]

2.7.6 The Role of African Elders in Conflict Resolution

Post-colonialism effects on the African continent have not been met without difficulty, where countries are struggling to deal with the independence and governance required.[96] Some challenges are where the inhabitants attempt to access justice in an inherited formal legal system designed to exclude them, even by language, which creates the biggest barrier. Thankfully with the aid of ADR processes, which are historically and inherently African, the divide can be crossed smoothly.[97] It becomes incumbent on Africa to within its governance, tap into its rich heritage, and align its customary practices towards conflict resolution. The customary practice of allowing the elder to resolve conflict is still practised and deeply ingrained in the African culture. In assessing this practice, one understands that this practice is still rife in Ethiopia, and they were not even colonised.[98] Rwanda, notwithstanding their colonisation, still utilised the Gacaca processes, which aided in customary conflicts.[99] In Botswana, they have their customary disputes parallel with the formal legal system, and the decision of the chief goes to the customary appeal court, where appeal court status is equivalent to the High Court.[100] SA is also a country that has afforded the rights of recognition to its traditional leaders, and affords chieftaincy its place of authority as decisions taken by the chief are recognised in SA law and implemented through customary law. Africa embraces its traditional customs, rituals, leaders and incorporates this into their legal system, to benefit the community they serve.

2.7.7 Conclusion

The African people's cultural customs, values, and practices place great value on community and social cohesion, where their elders are recognised as custodians and implementers. The emphasis on the religious standing of elders has allowed them to respect those devout to the vocation to mediate disputes without hesitation. The community surrenders to the decisions with little resistance and a spirit of

[95] Bosman (2014), p. 326.

[96] Adefisoye and Bamidele (2018), pp. 3–17.

[97] Ntuli (2018), p. 37.

[98] Kariuki (2015), p. 9.

[99] Kariuki (2015), p. 4.

[100] Kariuki (2015), pp. 4–5.

compromise and acceptance.[101] The African people built their communities on the communal understanding of *'ubuntu'*, which means 'I am because you are.'[102] The concept of *ubuntu* allows one to understand that everything you do has an effect and impact on your fellow man, and you need one another to survive, so a lot of reliance is placed on teamwork.[103] In following the *ubuntu* doctrine, a dispute is not resolved from the individual but rather for peace within the community.[104]

In Africa, the ADR processes have resonated well with its population, even though some still favour the rigour of the court system. ADR processes are often promoted as vehicles for facilitating access to justice based on common human principles of human dignity, restorative justice and equity.[105] The current understanding of access to justice conceptualises this principle as accessibility and fairness in the legal process itself.[106] The lack of resources may hinder access to justice, and this challenge is real for the African population, where many parts of Africa are still impoverished due to being plagued with corruption, political instability and civil unrest.[107]

2.7.8 Recommendations

The concept of *'ubuntu'* resonates with the African and is found within the rich African heritage.[108] Justice on the African continent can easily be accessed knowing these principles form the foundation of the ADR system and will be used in resolving domestic and international conflicts.[109] The role of the elder in conflict management and resolution can never be devalued as it requires experience, a level of high moral ethics, in a display of character that the individual must possess.[110] The mediator must always display a certain level of expertise to resolve the conflict.

ADR has always presented itself as a viable vehicle for access to justice that is convenient, easily understood in the native tongue and cost-effective for the poor African population. The only challenge of Africa is to bring its infrastructure up to speed, but luckily investment on that front is on the rise, and this will aid Africa to deal with ODR on a technological platform. It is recommended that Africa seeks

[101] Price (2018), p. 400.
[102] Ononogbu (2015), p. 86.
[103] Ononogbu (2015), p. 86.
[104] Ononogbu (2015), p. 86.
[105] Nolan-Haley (2020).
[106] Albertstein and Cohen (2019), pp. 1–41.
[107] Herbert Smith Freehills (2016), p. 5.
[108] Herbert Smith Freehills (2016), p. 5.
[109] Ononogbu (2015), p. 78.
[110] Ononogbu (2015), p. 78.

exciting and innovative ways to partner with investors who see the potential for growth and implement these technologies that serve the previously disadvantaged.

References

Abedi F et al (2019) Universal standards for the concept of fairness in online dispute resolution in B2C E-disputes. Ohio State J Dispute Resolution 34:357–392

Adefisoye TO, Bamidele O (2018) Africa: understanding and managing violent conflicts. Conflict Stud Q Issue 22:3–17

Albertstein M, Cohen H (2019) Multilevel access to justice in a world of vanishing trials: a conflict resolution perspective. Fordham Urban Law J 47:1–41

Bemmels B (1991) Arbitration theory and discipline arbitration. Ind Labor Relat Rev 44(3): 548–562

Blankley KM et al (2010) Multijurisdictional ADR practice: lessons for litigators. Cordoza J Conflict Resol 21:29–80

Blignaut C (2018) The effectiveness of conciliation as an alternative dispute resolution process in unfair dismissal disputes. Dissertation, University of Pretoria

Bookman PK (2019) The arbitration-litigation paradox. Va Law Rev 72(4):1119–1196

Bookman PK (2021) Arbitral courts. Va J Int Law 61(2):161–220

Bosman L (2014) The PCA's contribution to international dispute resolution in Africa. Stellenbosch Law Rev 25(2):308–327

Browning R (2017) South Africa as a preferred arbitration venue on the horizon? Without prejudice 22–24

Chowdhury JA (2016) ADR in criminal cases and decriminalisation of violence: a gender perspective. Indian J Law Justice 7(2):1–19

Christensen D (2014) Conciliation, uniqueness and rational toxicity. Wiley Periodicals, Inc, New York, pp 584–603

Cohen H, Alberstein M (2019) Multilevel access to justice in a world of vanishing trials: a conflict resolution perspective. Fordham Urban Law J 47(1):1–42

Comella VF (2014) Arbitration, democracy and the rule of law: some reflections on Owen Fiss's theory. University Pompeu Fabra, Barcelona, pp 1–33

Deutsch DS (1990) Litigate and arbitrate: a hybrid method of alternative dispute resolution. Comp Law J 10(4):517–550

Duursma A (2014) A current literature review of international mediation. Int J Confl Manag 25(1): 81–98

Fahimeh A et al (2019) Universal standards for the concept of fairness in online dispute resolution in B2C E-disputes. Ohio State J Dispute Resol 34(2):357–392

Gonzalez AG (2003) Ebay law: the legal implications of the C2C electronic commerce model. Comp Law Secur Rev:1–13

Greco AP (2010) ADR and a smile: neocolonialism and the West's newest export in Africa. Pepperdine Dispute Resol Law J 10(3):649–676

Harvey PE (1998) ADR: an evolutionary process. Advocate (Vancouver Bar Association) 56(4): 545–550

Herbert Smith Freehills (2016) A Multi-jurisdictional Review: Dispute Resolution in Africa Legal Guide 2nd ed 1–9; 266–270

Howard J, Graham S (1982) Conciliation - new beginnings? Probat J 29:87–92

Hyman JM (2015) Beyond fairness: the place of moral foundations theory in mediation and negotiation. Nevada Law J 15:959–981

Jacobs S, Aakhus M (2002) What mediators do with words: implementing three models of rational discussion in dispute mediation. Confl Resolut 20:177–183

Kariuki F (2015) Conflict resolution by elders in Africa: successes, challenges and opportunities. Chartered Institute of Arbitrators Centenary Conference Learning from Africa, Victoria Falls Convention Centre, Livingstone, Zambia, 15th July 2015

Kermez R (2010) Stages of the mediation process. Advanced mediation 1–18

Kopec M, Titelbaum MG (2016) The uniqueness thesis. Philos Compass 11:189–200

Marcello G (2010) From conflict to conciliation and Back again: some notes on Ricoeur's dialectic. Revista Filosophica de Coimbra 28:341–366

Mell J, Gratch J (2016) Interactive arbitration guide online. Proceedings of the 15th International Conference on Autonomous Agents and Multiagent Systems, May 9–13

Mojtaba D, Afshin AK (2018) Rethinking the use of deference in investment arbitration: new solutions against the perception of bias. UCLA J Int Law Foreign Aff 22:38–68

Nelson DW (2000) Overview - ADR in the 21st century: opportunities and challenges. Dispute Resol Magazine 6(3):3–5

Nolan-Haley J (2020) International dispute resolution and access to justice: comparative law perspectives. J Disput Resolut 398(2):391–412

Noll DE (2007) Mediation, then mediation -deeper dimensions. Dispute Resol Magazine 37

Ntuli N (2018) Africa: alternative dispute resolution in a comparative perspective. Conflict Stud Q Iss 22:36–80

Nwazi J (2017) Assessing the efficacy of alternative dispute resolution (ADR) in the settlement of environmental disputes in The Niger Delta region of Nigeria. J Law Conflict Resol 9:26–41

Olufemi A et al (2019) Dispute resolution within/between religious Organisations in Nigeria: litigation or alternative dispute resolution? Univ Gambia Law Rev:6–18

Ononogbu I (2015) Transformation of dispute resolution in Africa. Int J online Dispute Resol 2:77–87

Ordor A, Aiyedun A (2016) Integrating the traditional with the contemporary in dispute resolution in Africa. Law Democracy Dev 20:154–173

Parker RM, Hagin LJ (1993) ADR techniques in the reformation model of civil dispute. SMU Law Rev 46:1905–1933

Paulsson J (2010) Arbitration in three dimensions. 2:1–34

Peruginell G (2002) Artificial intelligence in alternative dispute resolution *Presentazione al Convegno lea workshop* 2002, bologna- July 13th, 2002

Porteous D (2018) The case for reframing ODR in emerging economies. Int J Online Dispute Resolution 5(1–2):61–68

Price C (2018) Alternative dispute resolution in Africa: is ADR the bridge between traditional and modern dispute resolution? Pepperdine Dispute Resol Law J:1–395

Reif L (2007) The use of Conciliation or mediation for the resolution of international commercial disputes. Int Commercial Disputes Conciliation Mediation:20–47

Revesz PZ (2014) Arbitration solutions to bargaining and game theory problems. Ann Univ Sci Budapest Sect Comp 42:21–38

Roberge JF, Fraser V (2019) Access to commercial justice: a roadmap for online dispute resolution (ODR) Design for Small and Medium-Sized Businesses (SMEs) disputes. Ohio State J Dispute Resol 35:1–62

Schmitz SJ (2001) What should we teach in ADR courses: concepts and skills for lawyers representing clients in mediation. Harv Negotiation Law Rev 6:189–210

Smith ND (1978) A warmer way of disputing: mediation and conciliation. Am J Comp Law 26: 205–216

Teper L (1949) The function of Management in Achieving Sound Labor Relations. Ind Labor Relat Rev 2:558–575

Terris LG, Maoz Z (2005) Rational mediation: a theory and a test. J Peace Res 42:565–583

Turner WC (2010) A brief overview of the use of evidence in arbitration. Nevada Lawyer 21–25

Verbeek PP (2012) Expanding the mediation theory, vol 17. Springer Science & Business Media Found Sci, Berlin, pp 391–395

Waincymer JM (2020) Online arbitration. Indian J Arbitr Law 9(1):1–23

Wanis-St JA (2000) Implementing ADR in transitioning states: lessons learned from practice. Harv Negotiation Law Rev 5:339–382
Wenying W (2005) The role of conciliation in resolving disputes: a P.R.C. Perspective. Ohio State J Dispute Resol 2:421–450
Yuksel AEB (2007) Online international arbitration. Ankara Law Rev 4:83–93

Khanyisa Kim Mgwenyana is an admitted Advocate of the High, she obtained her LLB degree at the University of Port Elizabeth. Her LLM degree in University of Pretoria (UP) and is currently completing her Doctoral Degree in Alternative Dispute Resolution at UP. She started off her career as a Public Prosecutor in both the District and Regional Courts of Johannesburg & Cape Town. She then moved into Government and worked in the Provincial Administration of the Western Cape, as a State Law Advisor. She chose to divert and specialise in Labour Law. She was then appointed as a Deputy Director, responsible for Labour Relations transversally, until she took up a position in the Commission for Conciliation, Mediation & Arbitration (CCMA) as a Part-Time Commissioner. She is currently employed at the Public Service Commission overseeing the Constitutional values and principles within the public service of South Africa.

Chapter 3
An Evaluation of International Commercial Arbitration Theories

Tshepo Twala

3.1 Introduction

This chapter explores different theories of international commercial arbitration with the aim of determining the theory that encapsulates the South African international commercial arbitration system. The study of international commercial arbitration theories in South Africa has been moderately scant, thus resulting in the restriction of the theoretical base in South Africa's international commercial arbitration framework.[1] In this regard, several historical and contemporary theories that may enhance the South African international commercial arbitration framework as a successful process of resolving international commercial disputes are assessed in order to address the aforementioned restricted theoretical base.[2]

This chapter explains the distinct interpretation of the nature of international commercial arbitration by juxtaposing different theories of international commercial arbitration. In this regard, four theories are discussed, namely: the jurisdictional theory; the contractual theory; the party autonomy and delocalisation theory; and the hybrid theory.[3] The evaluation of each of these theories is canvassed by considering: (i) the disposition of international commercial arbitration and its interconnection with national laws; (ii) the disposition and purview of the powers of an arbitrator in international commercial arbitration; and (iii) the status of arbitration awards under

This chapter is based on the LLM mini dissertation of the author T Tshepo which is available on the UP repository.

[1] Yu (2008), pp. 255–283. Please note that the author is not aware of any South African study that has considered theories of arbitration.

[2] Yu (2008), pp. 255–283.

[3] Yu (2008), p. 257.

T. Twala (✉)
University of Pretoria, Pretoria, South Africa

R. Baboolal Frank (ed.), *Dispute Resolution within Africa*,
https://doi.org/10.1007/978-3-031-76261-1_3

each theory in respect of the enforceability of international commercial arbitration awards. The following section of this chapter provides an overview of international commercial arbitration theories.

The arbitration discourse has mainly focused on which process is a cut above and the appraisal of arbitration outcomes thereto.[4] As such, many arbitration academics have come up with progressive steps to revitalise the development of arbitration theory and put it forward to legal practitioners' attention.[5] However, it is evident from reading the literature relating to the arbitration discourse that a theory of arbitration generally accepted as describing the South African international commercial arbitration system in a succinct and nuanced manner is yet to be determined.[6] It is therefore important to assess several theories of arbitration with the aim of determining the theories that succinctly encapsulate the South African international commercial arbitration framework, which will help South Africa gain some positive traction towards changing the perceptions of stakeholders and role players in the international commercial arbitration market.[7]

Some arbitration theorists assert that there are two main categories of international commercial arbitration theories, namely the judicial and political theories.[8] The judicial wing of the international commercial arbitration theories suggests that a "just" panacea of a dispute exists, and that it is the responsibility of an arbitrator to adjudge on the facts and principles involved in a dispute.[9] In the judicial theoretical paradigm, it is argued that an arbitrator is appointed to make rulings in respect of the economic interests and the legal rights of the parties involved, as contained in the information provided by the parties during the arbitration proceedings. On the other hand, the political wing of the international commercial arbitration theories views arbitration as an extension of both collective bargaining and collective coercion.[10] In the political theoretical paradigm, it is argued that one of the functions of an arbitrator is to accurately inscribe the respective strengths of the parties' merits and ensure that 'the lion gets his share'.[11] This argument is similar to the notion of compromise that is a core feature in conciliation and, although the notion of compromise may have a guidance role in arbitration proceedings, an arbitration process requires the decision of an outsider in respect of the merits of a dispute rather than an accommodation of the parties themselves (except in instances whereby parties initiate negotiation and the outcomes of such negotiation are made the award). An international commercial arbitration system that is firmly grounded on

[4]Carbonneau et al. (2016), pp. 1–500. See also Carnevale (1992), pp. 387–390.

[5]Carbonneau et al. (2016), pp. 1–500. See also Carnevale (1992), pp. 387–390.

[6]Saghir and Nyombi (2016), pp. 269–276. See also Yu (2008), pp. 255–286.

[7]Saghir and Nyombi (2016), pp. 269–276. See also Yu (2008), pp. 255–286; Moses (2017), pp. 1–392.

[8]Yu (2008), p. 257. See also Carlston (1952), pp. 631–651.

[9]Filippo (2018), pp. 1–200.

[10]Mattli and Dietz (2014), pp. 5–272.

[11]Schultz (2019), pp. 1–28.

the political theory may therefore be less preferable to both parties in a dispute, notwithstanding the obvious practicality of compromise from one instance to another.

In terms of the contractual theory, it is contended that international commercial arbitration emanates from a valid arbitration agreement between parties to a dispute and, as such, it must be coordinated or managed in a manner that accords with the wishes of the parties in dispute.[12] It argues that, in lieu of attaching international commercial arbitration into the national laws applicable to arbitration proceedings, international commercial arbitration should be treated as an autonomous institution and should not be controlled by the applicable national laws to arbitration proceedings.[13] This is to ensure that parties have unbridled autonomy to determine the manner in which their arbitration proceedings should be managed.[14] Contrastingly, the delocalisation theory endorses the view that arbitration proceedings must be free from the seat of arbitration's national legal framework.[15] On the other hand, the jurisdictional theory is premised on the notion that states must have complete supervisory powers to regulate all arbitration proceedings conducted in their jurisdiction.[16] However, the hybrid theory is a nexus between the jurisdictional theory and the contractual theory in that it advances the argument that international commercial arbitration has both a contractual character and a jurisdictional character, which coexist in harmony despite different ideologies or interests.[17] The next section of this chapter unpacks the aforementioned theories of international commercial arbitration.

3.2 Unpacking the Theories of International Commercial Arbitration

3.2.1 *The Jurisdictional Theory*

The jurisdictional theory brings to light the importance of states' supervisory powers, especially the supervisory powers of a state in respect of an arbitration taking place within the relevant state's jurisdiction. Jurisdictional theorists contest that the validity of an arbitration award must be decided upon based on the laws of the country where the enforcement or recognition of such an arbitration award is pursued.[18] Jurisdictional theorists also submit that the validity of an arbitration

[12] Yu (2008), p. 265. See also Romeyn (1980), pp. 181–195.

[13] Yu (2008), p. 265.

[14] Yu (2008), p. 265.

[15] Saghir and Nyombi (2016), p. 269.

[16] Amerasinghe (2011), pp. 10–284.

[17] Roberts (2014), pp. 1–70.

[18] Bantekas (2015), pp. 1–35.

agreement, together with the applicable arbitration procedure thereto, must be governed by the national laws of the seat where an arbitration takes place.[19] The proponents of the jurisdictional theory submit that all arbitration proceedings must be governed by the legal rules of the place where an arbitration is conducted and/or the parties' choice of law set out in their arbitration agreement.[20] These proponents state that arbitrators bear a resemblance to judges in courts of law because they draw their powers from the national laws of a state. Jurisdictional theorists advance that arbitrators, as is the case with judges in courts of law, have an obligation to apply the legal rules of the relevant state when settling the disputes before them.[21] Furthermore, the jurisdictional theory also argues that arbitration awards have a similar effect and status as a judgment in national courts.[22] On this score, jurisdictional theorists propound that arbitration awards should be enforced by the national courts of the place where such an enforcement or recognition is pursued, as is the case with judgments passed by the national courts of various jurisdictions.[23]

Jurisdictional theorists hold strong emphasis on the significance of the place in which arbitration proceedings take place (the so-called *lex fori*).[24] In this regard, Mann, a jurisdictional theorist, expands on the significance of law of the place where an arbitration is conducted.[25] Mann's expansion is premised on the argument that each state is empowered to either accept or reject activities that are carried out within its jurisdiction.[26] On this premise, he contests that all arbitration proceedings are subject to the law of the place where such arbitration proceedings are conducted.[27] This contention has led jurisdictional theorists to submit that an arbitrator has an obligation to ensure that arbitration proceedings are conducted in line with the parties' arbitration agreement, provided that the law of the place in which an arbitration takes place permits such terms of engagement.[28] This is because an act contrary to the mandatory rules and the principles on which the national laws of the place of arbitration are based is considered to be unjustified and unlawful from a judicial perspective.[29]

The several challenges faced by parties in international commercial arbitration, such as arbitration procedures, the enforceability of arbitration awards, the powers of arbitrators and the validity of an arbitration agreement, have to be decided upon based on the mandatory rules and the principles on which the national laws

---

[19] Bantekas (2015), pp. 1–35.

[20] Belohlavek (2013), pp. 66–75.

[21] Sanders (1975), pp. 205–234.

[22] Sanders (1975), pp. 205–234.

[23] Seyalova (2019), pp. 1–5.

[24] Ferrari (2011), pp. 1–178.

[25] Mann (1983), pp. 245–246.

[26] Mann (1983), p. 245.

[27] Mann (1983), p. 245.

[28] Gaillard (2010), pp. 1–202.

[29] Yu (2008), pp. 258–265.

applicable to the arbitration proceedings are based.[30] If these issues are not decided upon within the parameters of the mandatory rules and the principles on which the national laws applicable to the arbitration proceedings are based, it means that arbitration awards stand the risk of not surviving the scrutiny of the national courts of the relevant jurisdiction.[31] The national courts of such jurisdictions wherein arbitration awards are to be enforced would also be reluctant to allow the enforcement of such arbitration awards.[32]

The proponents of the jurisdictional theory also bestow a firm argument in respect of national courts having supervisory powers over arbitration proceedings.[33] The Convention on the Recognition and Enforcement of Foreign Arbitral Awards[34] confirms such supervisory powers. In terms of Article V of the New York Convention, the arbitration procedures, the composition of authority in arbitration proceedings and the validity of arbitration agreements and arbitration awards have to be decided upon in terms of the law of the place where an arbitration is conducted.[35] The national courts of the place where enforcement or recognition of an arbitration award is required by a party can exercise supervisory powers over the validity of such an arbitration award if the enforcement of such an arbitration award would be against its mandatory rules and the principles on which the national laws applicable to the arbitration proceedings are based, or if the dispute is not arbitrable under its laws.[36]

The jurisdictional theorists submit that the jurisdiction over arbitration proceedings is based on three pillars in respect of the supervisory powers of the national courts where arbitration proceedings are conducted, namely: (i) an arbitrator has the power to make binding arbitration awards, which power stems from the state's delegation of its exclusive powers in respect of arbitration proceedings; (ii) an act is generally susceptible to the law of the place where such an act occurred, unless agreed otherwise by the parties and within the confines of the applicable laws; and (iii) the application of the law of the place in which an arbitration takes place and its courts are often more efficient than other legal systems.[37] In this regard, it can be argued that the supervisory powers of national courts over arbitration proceedings are, in practice, conferred by applicable law. By way of example, the jurisdiction of South African courts over international arbitration proceedings conducted in South Africa is provided for by article 6 under schedule 1 (read with section 6) of

---

[30] Paulsson (2017), p. 2.

[31] Paulsson (2017), p. 2.

[32] Paulsson (2017), p. 2.

[33] Yu (2008), p. 259.

[34] Convention on the Recognition and Enforcement of Foreign Arbitral Awards, 1958 (hereafter, New York Convention).

[35] New York Convention.

[36] Koch (2009), pp. 267–292.

[37] Samuel (1989), pp. 294–296.

the International Arbitration Act[38] which, *inter alia*, grants the national courts of South Africa jurisdiction in respect of certain functions that require supervision and/or arbitration assistance.[39]

It is also argued that arbitrability succinctly expresses the central features of national courts having jurisdiction over arbitration proceedings.[40] This argument is based on the notion that arbitrators can only deal with a dispute if the applicable law that the parties have opted to subject themselves to before the relevant arbitration proceedings permits.[41] This is fundamentally because the arbitrability of a dispute must always be assessed against the law of the place where the relevant arbitration proceedings are conducted in instances whereby the parties have not agreed to the applicability of the law of another jurisdiction in their arbitration agreement to regulate such arbitration proceedings.[42] As such, the parties before arbitration proceedings may institute proceedings before the relevant national courts in order to challenge any concerns they may have regarding their arbitration proceedings, for example, where an arbitrator allows a dispute that is beyond the scope of arbitrability under the laws governing the arbitration proceedings to be arbitrated.[43]

Mann argues that, as is the case with procedural matters, the substantive issues of the dispute are also governed by national laws.[44] He remarked as follows in this regard:

No one has ever or anywhere been able to point to any provision or legal principle which permit[s] individuals to act outside the confines of a system of [national] law; even the idea of the autonomy of the parties exists only by virtue of a given system of [national] law and in different systems may have different characteristics and effects. Similarly, every arbitration is necessarily subject to the law of a given [s]tate. No private person has the right or the power to act on any level other than that of [national] law. Every right or power a private person enjoys is inexorably conferred by or derives from a system of [national] law which may conveniently and in accordance with tradition be called the [*lex fori*], though it would be more exact to speak of the [*lex arbitri*].[45]

Accordingly, as Mann articulates it, any compositions of arbitration tribunals and structures of arbitration proceedings are obliged to subject themselves to the national laws of the jurisdictions in which such arbitration tribunals and structures are based, unless there is an exemption system from such requirements.[46] Within the international commercial arbitration framework, only the national laws of the place in

[38] International Arbitration Act 15 of 2017 (hereafter, International Arbitration Act).

[39] International Arbitration Act article 6 under schedule 1.

[40] Mistelis and Brekoulakis (2009), pp. 1–375.

[41] Mrotzek (2017), pp. 1–62.

[42] Bermann (2012), pp. 367–378.

[43] Bantekas (2008), pp. 193–223.

[44] Mann (1983), p. 245.

[45] Mann (1983), p. 245.

[46] Mann (1983), p. 246.

which an arbitration is conducted can provide an efficacious and complete control over arbitration proceedings in order to decide both the relevant substantive and procedural matters that may arise during such proceedings.

3.2.2 *The Contractual Theory*

It is often argued that, notwithstanding the considerations of compulsory arbitration and arbitrability, the interconnection between the parties and arbitrators before arbitration proceedings is based on a contractual relationship.[47] This contractual relationship can be described as two-fold: (i) the contract between the parties which, in this case, is the arbitration agreement agreed to by the parties; and (ii) the agreement between the parties to appoint an arbitrator for their arbitration proceedings.[48] This categorisation means that a valid arbitration agreement between the parties must exist in order to initiate arbitration proceedings as well as an appointment agreement from the parties in order to ensure that the appointment of the relevant arbitrator is valid.[49] Upon the conclusion of the aforementioned contracts, a dispute between parties can be brought before an arbitrator who is then entrusted to preside before the arbitration proceedings and ensure that the dispute is appropriately finalised.[50]

The exponents of the contractual theory do not accord significance to the law of the place where arbitration proceedings are conducted or national laws that govern arbitration proceedings by operation of law but, instead, they contest that arbitration proceedings are, in fact, governed by the arbitration agreement concluded by the parties.[51] In this regard, contractual theorists argue that there are no strong ties between arbitration proceedings and the law of the place in which such an arbitration is conducted.[52] In their view, parties before the arbitration proceedings have the prerogative to decide on issues pertaining to their arbitration proceedings and this prerogative must not be impinged upon by the powers created by any national laws.[53] As such, in terms of the contractual theory, the resolution of a dispute before arbitration proceedings should not be influenced by national laws of the relevant jurisdiction and the principle of sanctity of contracts must prevail, free from any state influence.[54] In this regard, Kellor states that:

[47] Yu (2008), pp. 265–266.

[48] Please note that the appointment agreement between the parties can sometimes be incorporated as a clause and annexure in an arbitration agreement.

[49] Dodge and Pollman (2003), pp. 289–312.

[50] Escher and Krueger (2003), pp. 12–16.

[51] Yu (2008), p. 266.

[52] Rakoff and Rakoff (2019), pp. 13–22.

[53] Yu (2008), p. 266.

[54] Yu (2008), p. 266.

[A]rbitration is wholly voluntary in character. The contract of which the arbitration clause is a part is a voluntary agreement. No law requires the parties to make such a contract, nor does it give one party power to impose it on another. When such an arbitration agreement is made part of the principal contract, the parties voluntarily forgo established rights in favour of what they deem to be the greater advantages of arbitration.

Accordingly, with the exceptions of arbitrability and public policy which are reserved for the *lex fori*, the *lex fori* has very little influence over the procedures and outcome of the arbitration. Moreover, it has been concluded that 'national arbitration laws are only to supplement and fill lacunae in the parties' agreement as to the arbitration proceedings and to provide a code capable of regulating the conduct of an arbitration.[55]

Kellor's argument demonstrates that the contractual theory, in contrast to the jurisdictional theory, investigates the nature and function of arbitration processes from a contractual perspective.[56] In terms of the available literature, it is apparent that contractual theorists concede that arbitration processes have the potential to be influenced by applicable national laws, however, there is insistence on the argument that arbitration has a contractual disposition which stems from an arbitration agreement between parties.[57]

International commercial arbitration is largely configured on the contractual theory in most jurisdictions around the world.[58] The national courts of most jurisdictions gravitate towards the contractual theory and the relationship between an arbitrator and the parties is interpreted as one that is contractual in nature. This is amplified by the belief that this theoretical framework recognises the interests of businesses and their desire to have a more informal and flexible form of resolving disputes.[59] In England, the case of *Cereals S.A. v. Tradax Export SA*[60] is a good case study that depicts how national courts hold the contractual theory as crucial in the international commercial arbitration context. In this case, the court held that an arbitrator becomes a party to an arbitration agreement when such an arbitrator accepts the appointment to preside over such proceedings and must adhere to the terms of engagement set out in such an arbitration agreement.[61]

Amongst contractual theorists, there is also an issue regarding the nature of arbitration awards which centres around the agent theory. The proponents of the agent theory, such as Merlin and Foelix, argue that an arbitration award is a contract made by an arbitrator who acts as an agent of the parties before the arbitration

---

[55] Klein (1955), pp. 52–53.

[56] Klein (1955), pp. 1–320.

[57] Yu (2008), pp. 265–278.

[58] Weiskopf (2012), pp. 1–672.

[59] Yu (2008), pp. 265–278.

[60] *Cie Europeene de Cereals SA v. Tradax Export SA* 1986 2 *Lloyd's Rep.* U.K. 301.

[61] Yu (2008), p. 266.

proceedings.[62] Viewed from the perspective of an agent-principal relationship, the 'contract' made by the agent (an arbitrator) has a binding effect on the principals (being the parties).[63] Therefore, it is argued that the parties are obliged to accept the arbitration award as a contractually binding instrument between the parties and to give effect to it.[64] The contractual and/or agent theorists contest that such a contractual agreement demands that an arbitration award must be enforced by the parties in any jurisdiction where such an arbitration award may require recognition or enforcement.[65]

It is advanced that the concerns around territoriality must not come to the fore and that an arbitration award must be recognised and enforced as a contract in any jurisdiction because there is no state authority or power that should vest in international commercial arbitration proceedings.[66] Concurring with Merlin's view, Niboyet states that the contractual nature of arbitration awards stems from the fact that the authority of an arbitrator in a particular arbitration proceeding is derived from the parties' arbitration agreement, as opposed to the judicial authorities or national laws.[67] However, Klein, Bernard and Pallieri have made some attempts to counter Merlin's contention that an arbitration award is a contract moulded by the arbitrating parties, through their agent (an arbitrator).[68] Pallieri argues that it is not necessary to place arbitration awards into a particular juridical category, while Klein and Bernard state that an arbitration award is a by-product of the contractual relationship between an arbitrator and the parties in that "*an arbitration award is the work of the arbitrators*".[69] Therefore, it is arguable that the parties simply undertake that an arbitration award will be binding upon them and, in light of such an obligation agreed to by the parties, the national courts of the relevant jurisdictions will simply be required to recognise or enforce the relevant arbitration award—arbitrators therefore do not act as agents of the parties, but as presiding officers before the parties arbitration proceedings.

3.2.3 The Party Autonomy and Delocalisation Theory

Party autonomy is defined as the representation of a party's free will when entering into a contract, while delocalisation is a theory which argues that the arbitration

[62] Merlin (1829), p. 34.

[63] Foelix and Demangeat (2013), pp. 1–318.

[64] Merlin (1829), p. 34.

[65] Foelix and Demangeat (2013), pp. 1–318.

[66] Yu (2008), p. 272.

[67] Niboyet (1950), p. 137.

[68] Klein (1955), pp. 1–320. See also Bernard (1937), p. 28; Pallieri (1935), pp. 287–311.

[69] Klein (1955), pp. 1–320. See also Bernard (1937), p. 28; Pallieri (1935), pp. 287–311.

system must be free from the surveillance of national laws.[70] The proponents of a delocalised arbitration submit that arbitration proceedings regulate themselves without external influence, which affords the parties in arbitration proceedings an opportunity to set their procedural rules and abide by them.[71] According to delocalisation theorists, delocalisation creates room for disputes to be resolved by way of a common understanding and mutual support between parties and arbitration institutions.[72] On the basis of this model, delocalisation proponents contend that there is no need for judicial intervention in arbitration proceedings because parties agree to resolve disputes in a manner that is compliant with the arbitration processes autonomously agreed to by the parties.[73] Delocalisation espouses the view that arbitration proceedings must be supra-national, and that the national laws of the relevant jurisdiction must not have power or control over arbitration processes.[74]

It is therefore unsurprising that the delocalisation scholarship raises concerns over judicial intervention that takes place over arbitration proceedings, akin to the contractual theory albeit from a different perspective.[75] Delocalisation theorists contend that the arbitration system must be wholly independent and free from judicial intervention.[76] Although this contention may seem attractive to some persons, it is very difficult to give empirical substance to this theoretical standpoint without an arbitration appeal or review structure in place. In this regard, it is often questioned whether a thinned-out form of delocalisation is possible and, if so, the kind of model that it would adopt.[77] As part of the solution-finding process, the core objective of this section is essentially to investigate the evolution of the delocalisation theory, with a distinct focus around the limitation of judicial intervention in arbitration proceedings.

Given the fact that privacy is one of the core principles of arbitration, delocalisation theorists also argue that the affiliation of the arbitration system with judicial oversight is antithetical because intervention by national courts undermines the aforementioned core principle of arbitration, amongst others.[78] Notwithstanding this point, it is apparent that legal scholars and practitioners have started to appreciate the national laws' non-controlling function in that the national courts' role in arbitration proceedings is now viewed as being a support structure to the arbitration system, as opposed to a controlling role.[79]

[70] Dursun (2012), pp. 161–186. See also Saghir and Nyombi (2016), p. 269.

[71] Perepelynska (2012), p. 38.

[72] Redfern et al. (2004), pp. 1–661.

[73] Pryles (2008), pp. 1–6.

[74] Li (2011), pp. 1–6.

[75] Saghir and Nyombi (2016), p. 275.

[76] Pryles (2008), pp. 1–6.

[77] Saghir and Nyombi (2016), p. 276.

[78] Berger (2015), pp. 1–992.

[79] Saghir and Nyombi (2016), pp. 269–276.

While delocalised arbitration may be an ideal concept, legal scholars and practitioners regard it as a far-fetched reality.[80] The main critique around delocalisation is that it is "wholly unrealistic", with the critics describing delocalisation as an attempt to create a 'legal vacuum' in arbitration proceedings.[81] Redfern and Hunter contend that delocalisation is a deceptive theoretical framework because, in their view, the national laws of the place where an arbitration is conducted should govern or regulate such arbitration proceedings, including the national laws of the jurisdiction where a party seeks the enforcement of an arbitration award.[82] This contention is also supported by Mann who argues that delocalisation is impractical because every right that a person is entitled to inexorably attains its heart beat from a system of national laws and, as such, all arbitration proceedings must be subject to the national laws of a given state.[83] In this regard, the proponents of the delocalisation theory contest that delocalisation must not be viewed as an attempt to evade the legal regime of any jurisdiction.[84] Instead, the delocalisation theory should be understood as a contestation that national laws must not impose limits or parameters on how arbitrations should be conducted, which will ensure that all arbitration proceedings are extricated from the confines of the national laws of the place where an arbitration is conducted.[85]

The critics of the delocalisation theory argue that it is imperative to maintain judicial oversight over arbitration proceedings in order to safeguard each country's justice system by keeping track of the quality of decisions made by arbitrators.[86] On this score, it is argued that judicial oversight is undoubtably justifiable and important for the purposes of inoculating national commercial or jurisdictional interests.[87] The idea of having arbitration processes that are distinct from national laws and without any judicial oversight carries the possibility of damaging the feasibility of arbitration proceedings—there must be a delicate balance between the arbitration jurisprudence and party autonomy principles in order to avoid the possibility of such a compromise. In this regard, article 11(4) of the UNCITRAL Model Law on International Commercial Arbitration[88] provides a useful guideline by recognising the important function of national courts to ensure that arbitration proceedings do not reach an impasse. For the sake of completeness, article 11(4) of the UNCITRAL Model Law sets out the instances whereby judicial intervention may be required in respect of certain issues that arise prior, during or upon the conclusion of arbitration

[80] Tweeddale and Tweeddale (2007), pp. 1–1128.

[81] Li (2011), pp. 1–4.

[82] Redfern et al. (2015), p. 187.

[83] Mann (1967), p. 157.

[84] Saghir and Nyombi (2016), p. 271.

[85] Saghir and Nyombi (2016), p. 271.

[86] Park (2007), pp. 1–904.

[87] Park (2007), pp. 1–904.

[88] UNCITRAL Model Law on International Commercial Arbitration, 1985 as amended (hereafter, UNCITRAL Model Law).

proceedings.[89] It is therefore vital to afford parties an opportunity to seek judicial intervention where necessary, within the legal parameters permitted by the relevant jurisdiction.

In light of the contrasting views set out above, Saghir and Nyombi propose a solution that ensures that delocalisation and judicial oversight coexist in harmony in respect of arbitration proceedings.[90] Paulsson submits that the question that we should ask ourselves is whether the arbitration system can be unfettered from the local peculiarities of the place where arbitration proceedings are conducted.[91] On the other hand, Bucher states that, while he understands the legitimacy of Paulsson's contention, the primary objective behind the delocalisation of the arbitration system can rather be accomplished by parties connecting or aligning their arbitration proceedings to jurisdictions whereby the arbitration award made from such proceedings can be enforced in the relevant jurisdictions without hassle.[92] In Bucher's view, this kind of an approach will ensure that an arbitration award is not frivolously challenged, and also capture the veracious meaning of delocalisation in order to sensibly accomplish a delocalised arbitration system.[93]

Greenberg and Weermantry also provide an alternative solution to the predicament faced by the delocalisation theory and submit that a diluted version of the concept exists and should be considered in the absence of a pure delocalisation.[94] In this diluted version, it is argued that the national laws of the relevant jurisdictions must cater for a relaxed approach to arbitration proceedings occurring within their jurisdictions.[95] According to Greenberg and Weermantry, a relaxed approach with limited intervention of national law processes makes sense as it helps preserve the autonomy of the parties, while enforcing national laws where necessary in certain circumstances.[96] Therefore, instead of separating delocalisation from national laws with little to no success, it is better to have a diluted delocalisation version as it preserves the autonomy of the parties and ensures that national laws are enforced where required.

3.2.4 The Hybrid Theory

The jurisdictional and contractual theories have ample backing at antithetical ends of the arbitration spectrum, however, according to some jurists, neither the

[89] Article 11(4) of the UNCITRAL Model Law.

[90] Saghir and Nyombi (2016), p. 275.

[91] Paulsson (1983), pp. 53–54.

[92] Saghir and Nyombi (2016), p. 274.

[93] Saghir and Nyombi (2016), p. 274.

[94] Greenberg (2011), pp. 1–582.

[95] Greenberg (2011), pp. 1–582.

[96] Greenberg (2011), pp. 1–582.

jurisdictional theory nor the contractual theory explains the modern framework of international commercial arbitration in a logical and concise manner.[97] As Lew puts it, the development of a mixed or hybrid theory as a compromise theory is therefore not surprising.[98] The advocates of the hybrid theory are of the view that the ideal international commercial arbitration model hinges on both jurisdictional and contractual components, which explains why the hybrid theory is viewed as a compromise theory in that it is essentially a mix of both the contractual and jurisdictional theories.[99]

Sauser-Hall propounds that international commercial arbitration is an alternative dispute resolution mechanism with a binary composition because, on the one hand, it carries a contractual component of arbitration which is denoted in the reasoning that arbitration proceedings originated from a contract between the parties, where such parties derive their power to select an arbitrator to preside over their arbitration proceedings and also agree on the rules that govern the relevant arbitration proceedings.[100] On the other hand, Sauser-Hall submits that international commercial arbitration also carries a jurisdictional component in that arbitration proceedings must be conducted within the parameters of the applicable national laws in order to, *inter alia*, determine whether an arbitration agreement is valid and whether an arbitration award is enforceable.[101]

It is on the basis of the dual character nature of the hybrid or mixed theory that hybrid theorists define arbitration as "a mixed juridical institution, sui generis, which has its origin in the [parties'] agreement and draws its jurisdictional effects from the civil law".[102] Accordingly, arbitration proceedings derive their heartbeat from the arbitration agreement concluded by the parties, while the jurisdictional nature of arbitration proceedings stems from the application of national laws in such proceedings. Some practitioners, such as Redfern and Hunter, endorse Sauser-Hall's argument and expressly state that:

International commercial arbitration is... hybrid. It begins as a private agreement between the parties. It continues by way of private proceedings, in which the wishes of the parties are of great importance. Yet it ends with an award which has binding legal force and effect and which, on appropriate conditions being met, the courts of most countries of the world will be prepared to recognise and enforce. The private process has a public effect, implemented by the support of the public authorities of each state expressed through its national law.[103]

According to Sanders, the hybrid theory seems to be a better theoretical framework than the contractual theory or jurisdictional theory to address issues that

[97] Yu (2008), p. 274.

[98] Lew (1978), p. 53.

[99] Lew (1978), p. 57.

[100] Sauser-Hall (1952), pp. 1–469.

[101] Sauser-Hall (1952), pp. 1–469.

[102] Roberts (2014), pp. 1–70.

[103] Redfern et al. (2004), pp. 1–661.

concern arbitration proceedings.[104] In Sanders' view, this is because placing an emphasis on (or choosing) one element of the arbitration system (contractual or jurisdictional) would be inadequate.

Robert, who supports the dual nature of the arbitration system, submits that there is a contiguous connection between arbitration proceedings and the national laws of the place where an such an arbitration is conducted.[105] Robert explains that the make-up of arbitration proceedings and the powers of an arbitrator are rooted on the arbitration agreement concluded by the parties, while the determination on whether an arbitration agreement is valid and/or whether an arbitration award can be enforced has to be made in accordance with the national laws of the relevant jurisdiction.[106] Contrary to the contractual theory, the powers of an arbitrator are subject to the national laws and the public policy rules of the relevant jurisdiction.[107] In respect of the nature of the arbitration awards, the hybrid theory defines the sum and substance of arbitration awards as a combination of both a judicial component and a contractual component, which is also distinct from both the jurisdictional and contractual theories.[108]

3.3 Conclusion

This chapter demonstrated that it is imperative for South Africa to comprehend how international commercial arbitration functions from a theoretical perspective. From a South African perspective, the enactment of the International Arbitration Act and its adoption of the UNCITRAL Model Law is an indication of South Africa's standpoint being, to a large extent, grounded on the hybrid or mixed theory as it is a combination of both the jurisdictional theory and the contractual theory.

The principles of the jurisdictional theory and the contractual theory are endorsed by the UNCITRAL Model Law in that international commercial arbitration proceedings: (i) originate from a contract between the parties, where such parties derive their power to select an arbitrator to preside over their arbitration proceedings and also agree on the rules that govern the relevant arbitration proceedings; and (ii) they must be conducted within the parameters of the applicable national laws in order to, *inter alia*, determine whether an arbitration agreement is valid and whether an arbitration award is enforceable.[109] It is posited that the enactment of the International Arbitration Act and its adoption of the UNCITRAL Model Law is going to continue helping South Africa experience a progressive increase in the number of

[104] Yu (2008), p. 275.
[105] Yu (2008), pp. 276–277.
[106] Yu (2008), pp. 276–277.
[107] Grenig (2021), pp. 1–30.
[108] Yu (2008), pp. 276–278.
[109] Sauser-Hall (1952), pp. 1–469.

international commercial arbitration disputes that are brought to its jurisdiction and will also aid South Africa's quest to be a leading international commercial arbitration jurisdiction.[110]

The delocalisation theory is strongly criticised and has a lot of shortcomings in that only a few parties, if any, would not want to be bound to any national legal system and thereby compromise legal certainty over their arbitration proceedings. Practically, the success of international commercial arbitration proceedings lies in the successful enforcement of an arbitration award which can only be achieved if the relevant proceedings conform with applicable standards of international commercial arbitration. In contrast to the jurisdictional, contractual and hybrid theories, it is evident that the autonomous theory goes further on than the reality of modern international commercial arbitration. While both the jurisdictional and contractual theories take two antithetical positions on the same gamut, the hybrid theory is an important compromise that South Africa has developed over the years and it is a more generally acceptable and feasible theory of international commercial arbitration in most jurisdictions. Within the present international commercial arbitration framework, the yardstick for determining whether an arbitration award can be enforced is based on the relevant national laws of the jurisdiction where such enforcement is sought. As such, based on the fact that South Africa's international commercial arbitration comprises of this yardstick and the jurisdictional and contractual theories, it can be said that the hybrid theory is the theory that encapsulates the South African international commercial arbitration system in a succinct and nuanced manner.

South Africa has a contiguous connection between its arbitration proceedings and the national laws. The make-up of arbitration proceedings and the powers of an arbitrator in South Africa are rooted on the arbitration agreement concluded by the parties and the determination on whether an arbitration agreement is valid and/or whether an arbitration award is enforceable has to be determined in accordance with its national laws.[111] The enactment of the International Arbitration Act has helped South Africa align its international commercial arbitration framework to various jurisdictions via the UNCITRAL Model Law whereby arbitration awards made from international commercial arbitration proceedings subject to its national laws can be enforced in the various jurisdictions without hassle. This alignment and approach towards applying internationally accepted standards does help enhance the feasibility of international commercial arbitrations and it can be argued that the hybrid theory of arbitration encapsulates the South African international commercial arbitration system in a succinct and nuanced manner.

It is important for South Africa's arbitration scholarship to continue considering conflict dynamics involved in international commercial arbitration as they develop over time in order to keep improving South Africa's theoretical framework, to ensure that the South African international commercial arbitration system is constantly

[110]Wethmar-Lemmer and Schoeman (2019), p. 127.

[111]Wethmar-Lemmer and Schoeman (2019), p. 127.

working towards maximising its effectiveness and also foster change in the perception of South Africa lagging behind other leading jurisdictions.

References

Amerasinghe CF (2011) International arbitral jurisdiction. Martinus Nijhoff Publishers, Leiden

Arbitration Act 42 of 1965

Bantekas I (2008) The foundations of arbitrability in international commercial arbitration. Aust Yearb Int Law 27:193–223

Bantekas I (2015) An introduction to international arbitration. Cambridge University Press, New York

Belohlavek AJ (2013) Arbitration and basic rights: movement from contractual theory to jurisdictional theory. Universitas, Czechia

Berger KP (2015) Private dispute resolution in international business: negotiation, mediation and arbitration. Kluwer Law International, Alphen aan den Rijn

Bermann GA (2012) Arbitration fundamentals. Am Rev Int Arbitr 23:367–378

Bernard A (1937) Arbitrage volontaire en droit privé: l'arbitrage en droit interne belge et français, étude critique comparée, l'arbitrage en droit international privé, droit compare. Bruxelles, Brussels

Carbonneau TE et al (2016) AAA handbook on mediation. JurisNet, LLC, New York

Carlston S (1952) Theory of the arbitration process. Law Contemp Probl 17(4):631–651

Carnevale PJ (1992) The usefulness of mediation theory. Negot J 387

Cie Europeene de Cereals SA v. Tradax Export SA 1986 2 Lloyd's Rep. U.K. 301

Constitution of the Republic of South Africa, 1996

Convention on the Recognition and Enforcement of Foreign Arbitral Awards, 1958

Dodge JL, Pollman E (2003) Arbitration, consent and contractual theory: the implications of EEOC v. Waffle House. Harv Negotiation Law Rev 8:289–312

Dursun AGS (2012) A critical examination of the role of party autonomy in international commercial arbitration and an assessment of its role and extent. Yalova Üniversitesi Hukuk Fakültesi Dergisi 1:161–186

Escher S, Krueger K (2003) The cost of carry and prejudgment interest. Litigation Econ Rev 6:12–16

Ferrari F et al (2011) Conflict of laws in international arbitration. JurisNet, New York

Filippo F (2018) Jurisdiction and admissibility in investment arbitration (Brill research perspectives in international law). Brill Nijhoff, Leiden

Foelix JJG, Demangeat C (2013) Traité du Droit International Privé ou du Conflit des Lois de Différentes Nations en Matière de Droit Privé. Nabu Press, Charleston

Gaillard E (2010) Legal theory of international arbitration. Martinus Nijhoff Publishers, Leiden

Greenberg S, Kee C, Weeramantry JR (2011) International commercial arbitration: an Asia- Pacific perspective. Cambridge University Press, New York

Grenig JE (2021) International commercial arbitration. Thomson Reuters, Toronto

International Arbitration Act 15 of 2017

Klein FE (1955) Considérations sur l'arbitrage en droit international privé précédées d'une étude de législation, de doctrine et de jurisprudence comparées en la matière. Helbing & Lichtenhahn, Cham

Koch C (2009) The enforcement of awards annulled in their place of origin. J Int Arbitr 26(2): 267–292

Lew JDM (1978) Applicable law in international commercial arbitration: a study in commercial arbitration awards. Oxford University Press, Oxford

Li J (2011) The application of the delocalisation theory in current international commercial arbitration. Int Company Commercial Law Rev:1–6
Mann FA (1967) Lex Facit Arbitrum in Sanders, P International arbitration: Liber amicorum for Martin Domke
Mann FA (1983) Lex facit arbitrum. Arbitr Int 2(3):245–246
Mattli W, Dietz T (2014) International arbitration and global governance: contending theories and evidence. Oxford University Press, Oxford
Merlin PA (1829) Recueil alphabétique de questions de droit. BnF Gallica, Paris
Mistelis LA, Brekoulakis SL (2009) Arbitrability: international & comparative perspectives. Kluwer Law International, Alphen aan den Rijn
Moses ML (2017) The principles and practice of international commercial arbitration. Cambridge University Press, Cambridge
Mrotzek C (2017) The development of concept of arbitrability—an international comparison. Dissertation, University of Cape Town
Niboyet JP (1950) Traité de droit international privé francais. Cambridge University Press, Cambridge
Pallieri GB (1935) L'Arbitrage privé dans les rapports internationaux. Recueil des cours 51:287–311
Park WW (2007) Arbitration of international business disputes: studies in law and practice. Oxford University Press, Oxford
Paulsson J (1983) Delocalisation of international commercial arbitration: when and why it matters. Int Comp Law Q 32:53–61
Paulsson MRP (2017) Enforcement of annulled awards: A restatement for the New York Convention? Kluwer Arbitration Blog 2
Perepelynska OS (2012) Party autonomy vs. mandatory rules in international arbitration. Ukrainian J Bus Law:38–39
Pryles M (2008) Limits to party autonomy in arbitral procedure. Int Council Commercial Arbitr:1–6
Rakoff TD, Rakoff JS (2019) Arbitration, "pseudo-contract," and objective theory. Harv Law Rev Forum 133:13–22
Redfern A et al (2004) Law and practice of international commercial arbitration. Sweet & Maxwell, London
Redfern A et al (2015) Redfern and hunter on international arbitration. Oxford University Press, Oxford
Roberts A (2014) State-to-state investment treaty arbitration: a hybrid theory of interdependent rights and shared interpretive authority. Harv Int Law J 55(1):1–70
Romeyn J (1980) Towards a motivational theory of arbitration in Australia. J Ind Relat 22(2): 181–195
Saghir Z, Nyombi C (2016) Delocalisation in international commercial arbitration: a theory in need of practical application. Int Company Commercial Law Rev 8:269–276
Samuel A (1989) Jurisdictional problems in international commercial arbitration. A study of Belgian, Dutch, English, French, Swedish, USA and west German law, Zürich. The. Int Lawyer 24(1):294–296
Sanders P (1975) Trends in the field of international commercial arbitration. Recueil des cours 145(2):205–234
Sauser-Hall G (1952) L'arbitrage en droit international privé. Annuaire de l'Institut de droit international 1–469
Schultz T (2019) The ethos of arbitration. King's College London Law School Research Paper 23: 1–28
Seyalova N (2019) Foreign court judgments and international arbitration awards enforcement. Int In-house Counsel J 12(47):1–5
Tweeddale A, Tweeddale K (2007) Arbitration of commercial disputes: international and English law and practice. Oxford University Press, Oxford

UNCITRAL Model Law on International Commercial Arbitration 1985 with amendments as adopted in 2006
UNCITRAL Convention on the Recognition and Enforcement of Foreign Arbitral Awards (New York, 1958)
Wethmar-Lemmer M, Schoeman E (2019) The International Arbitration Act 15 of 2017: Impetus for developmentson the cross- border commercial front. Tydskrif vir die Suid-Afrikaanse Reg 1: 127–137
Weiskopf NR (2012) Commercial arbitration: theory and practice. Vandeplas Publishing, Florida
Yu HL (2008) A theoretical overview of the foundations of international commercial arbitration. Contemp Asia Arbitr J 1(2):255–286

Tshepo Twala is an associate at Bowmans in Banking and Financiale Services Regulatory department of the Johannesburg office. Tshepo is a financial sector-focused regulatory lawyer who specialises in financial services (including asset management), securities, fund management, domestic and international payment services, financial technology (fintech) services, regulated lending, exchange control, banking services and anti-money laundering and counter-terrorist financing.

He regularly advises financial service providers (including asset managers), capital market participants (such as exchanges, brokers, custodians and nominees), fund managers, domestic and international payment service providers, fintech service providers, regulated credit providers and banks on compliance matters, product distribution and marketing requirements, and on registration, licensing, authorisation and approval requirements.

Tshepo holds LLB and LLM degrees (both awarded with distinction) from the University of Pretoria.

Chapter 4
A Review of the Indigenous Methods of Resolving Problems for African Continental Issues

Matome Malatsi

4.1 Introduction

The subject of adopting indigenous methods of resolving problems for African continental issues is an appropriate and relevant discourse in modern days.[1] Many scholars posit that customary and formal justice systems are both constituents of pluralistic legal systems prevailing in many African communities, from which citizens can exercise a choice regarding methods to use for resolving their disputes.[2] The Indigenous methods of resolving conflict have always existed in Africa for many years and have been lauded for flexibility, efficiency and effectiveness in promoting harmony, peace and stability in traditional society as compared to the rigid Western formal justice system inherited after colonisation.[3] These less adversarial indigenous problem-solving methods are deeply rooted in customs and culture of peace in traditional communities, and are used to resolve various conflicts, including land disputes, disagreements regarding frontiers and family conflicts.[4]

African traditional communities are confronted with challenges such as poverty, conflict, underdevelopment, corruption among other challenges.[5] The prevalence of these challenges in African communities makes a case for the adoption of traditional dispute resolution methods to address them.

This chapter is premised on academic work by the author M Malatsi that is yet to be made available on the UP repository as part of the LLM mini dissertation.

[1] Abe and Ouma (2017), pp. 1–19.

[2] Pimentel (2011), p. 3.

[3] Oluduro (2011), p. 307.

[4] Okonkwo (2017), pp. 55–78.

[5] Annan (2014), pp. 1–16.

M. Malatsi (✉)
University of Pretoria, Pretoria, ZA, South Africa

R. Baboolal Frank (ed.), *Dispute Resolution within Africa*,
https://doi.org/10.1007/978-3-031-76261-1_4

The cultural dimension of the customary dispute resolution methods makes them unique and provides more impetus because community members will embrace them as they are more likely to relate well with their own custom and practices.[6] In these methods, there are valuable lessons to modern society in promoting active participation by communities in finding solutions for problems that affect them.[7]

African countries like Rwanda, Ghana, Kenya, and Mauritius among others, have shown growing interest in adopting traditional methods of resolving problems as they resonate with their values and customs to build stable and harmonious communities through reconciliation and healing.[8] Price shows how Ghana provides for a good example of how African communities can build on traditional problem-solving methods to make justice more accessible in a way that is efficient and effective.[9] This warrants examination of lessons learnt from Ghana and other countries on how the customary methods of resolving disputes were brought into the mainstream legal justice system. However, it must be mentioned that this customary approach to ADR has its own shortcomings.[10]

This essay aims to explain the strengths and weaknesses of adopting indigenous methods for resolving problems for African continental issues through analysis of the historical context, reflection on principles applicable, highlight some of the methods used and share some experiences of African countries that have used traditional dispute resolution methods to address challenges. Conclusion will indicate the value- add of the traditional dispute resolution methods to ADR and formal justice systems in African communities.

4.2 Historical Perspective of Indigenous Problem- Solving Methods in Africa

Indigenous methods are unwritten practices and customary principles for resolving disputes, established over the years, passed from one generation to the next, and used by the original inhabitants of the African continent in various communities in accordance with their culture, traditions and unique circumstances.[11] These methods which were embedded in African customs and traditions focused on resolving the disputes, reconciling the parties and promoting healing.[12] Culture plays a significant role to anchor the traditional dispute resolution mechanisms where social ties and

[6]Ajayi and Buhari (2014), pp. 138–155.

[7]Rammala (2021), pp. 219–241.

[8]Bosman and Kimani (2018), pp. 113–148.

[9]Price (2018), p. 147.

[10]Ibe and Abugu (2022a), pp. 36–49.

[11]Olaoba (2010), p. 25.

[12]Dieng (2011), p. 1.

bonds keep the community together.[13] The key focal point becomes the communal cultures where the people are bound by deep social relations, long existing special links, shared values and trust for one another, such that the level of allegiance to the community will be high amongst members of the community. Conflict will still present itself to such communities because it is a common phenomenon experienced amongst all African communities, as it is the case the world over.[14] The existing special bonds, norms and beliefs embedded in cultural practices are the ones that make it easier for the elders to operate as dispute resolution champions given their Knowledge and wisdom to resolve conflict in a manner that provides an opportunity for co-existence and restored relations.[15] Many scholars indicate that albeit conflict is a concept hard to define, it can be described as a condition that arises when two or more people have incompatible objectives as a result of differences in attitude, beliefs and needs for example.[16] For conflict to arise, Okwonko's exposition of border conflicts among most Northern African countries demonstrates that there must be certain people located within certain communities, be it religious, ethnic, socio-political, economic, cultural or otherwise, who are in stark opposition to one another in pursuit of contrary objectives.[17]

To gauge the efficiency and effectiveness of traditional dispute resolution methods including the benefits and shortcomings, it is necessary to highlight what entails the very challenges that confront African communities and how these methods were used in addressing them. Problems for African continental issues are challenges experienced by average African traditional communities in the realm of political, social, economic, and environmental spheres that affect the entire African continent, which give rise to conflict situations. The Institute for Security Studies (ISS) points out that quick response is needed to address the ongoing confrontation and political strife on the African continent to avoid disaster in countries like, among others, Ethiopia, Libya, Central African Republic and South Sudan.[18] Political instability is caused by factors such as tussles for authority between various groups, argued polls, and the failure of governance, including corruption.[19] Economic inequality is another factor that can contribute to conflict, as it can create tensions between different groups over access to resources and opportunities.[20] In addition, land disputes also confront many African countries.[21] Competition over natural resources, such as water, and minerals can also be a driver

[13] Kariuki (2015), p. 2.

[14] Bujo (1988), pp. 198–202.

[15] African Union Commission Report (2015).

[16] Abifarin et al. (2019), pp. 2–7.

[17] Okonkwo (2017), pp. 55, 62. See also Adefisoye and Africa (2018), pp. 3–4.

[18] ISS REPORT (2017).

[19] Annan (2014), pp. 1–16.

[20] The Ocean Data and Information Network for Africa (ODINAFRICA) Status Report on African Maritime Border Disputes (2014).

[21] Home (2020), pp. 72–92.

of conflict.[22] African continental issues also encompass challenges related to gender inequality, human rights abuses, armed conflicts, and the need for sustainable development.[23] These are just a few examples of the key factors that can contribute to conflicts in Africa. Addressing these issues may require efficient and effective conflict resolution mechanisms that stood the test of time.

Customary methods for resolving conflicts existed even before colonialism and were used by many villages and tribes in Africa as mechanisms to promote coherence, peace, and harmony in the community.[24] Price indicates that the advent of colonialism saw Western legal system being imposed in African communities, relegating the traditional methods to the background.[25] However, the traditional methods such as the concept of village justice persisted as traditional communities continued with their customary practice to meet under the tree and resolve their disputes through community consensus and restorative justice.[26] These informal customary practices are deeply rooted in the African traditions of allowing the community to attend the meeting and participate actively in finding solutions to the problems that affect them as a collective.[27] Africans find value in unity of purpose and solidarity.[28] The involvement of the whole community and allegiance to cultural practices and traditions, made all village members to be committed to the customary methods and to abide by the decisions issued against the perpetrators.[29] The recipients complied with the sentences because they respected their communities as well as the wisdom of the elders who presided over the disputes.[30] This bears testimony that the traditional dispute resolution methods are embedded in values, culture and traditions that brings all members of the community together, a matter which motivates for compliance with judgments.[31]

Abifarin explains that the customary processes to resolve conflict used a step by step approach following a particular escalation level, first the disputants will attempt to negotiate a settlement by themselves, if unsuccessful, they will seek the assistance of an elderly member of the community to facilitate their engagement to attain a resolution.[32] If there is still no positive outcome, the matter will be elevated to the Headman thereafter it will be taken to the Chief.[33] The Chief- in- council will play the role of the arbitrator to resolve the conflict, taking into account the interest of the

[22] Onigun and Albert (2001).
[23] Van der Waal (2006), p. 140.
[24] Oluduro (2011), p. 307.
[25] Price (2018), p. 396.
[26] Menkel-Meadow (2014).
[27] Osi (2008a), p. 163.
[28] Mandova (2013), pp. 100–108.
[29] Edzii (2018), p. 46.
[30] Olaoba (2001), p. 1.
[31] Pkalya et al. (2004), pp. 89–95.
[32] Abifarin et al. (2019), pp. 6–18.
[33] Ajayi and Buhari (2014), p. 143.

community and to foster reconciliation and healing.[34] The benefits of the method outlined is that it was accessible for disputants, affordable and allows for active participation by the community.[35] The enforcement of the award did not present difficulty because of community involvement and the licence to operate which is accorded to the elders as people with knowledge, experience and wisdom regarding the application of traditional dispute resolution methods. As a result, any condescending behaviour on compliance with the sanction meted by the elders will be scorned by the community.[36]

The traditional dispute resolution methods are guided by certain values and principles that have strong connections to African culture and traditions.[37] The typical principles are, amongst others, truth, forgiveness, social justice, coherence among the society, confidence in the ability of the elders, and mutual trust.[38] A disputant who sought intervention must be confident that the elders are capable of finding resolution of the dispute presented.[39] All the participants are required to be truthful and honest to ensure the process is credible and continues to finality.[40] Embedded in the norms and traditions of the communities, is the value of respect for seniors, the departed, families and fellow citizens and that is prescribed by usage and passed from generations to generations.[41]

4.3 Discussion of Indigenous Problem- Solving Methods for African Issues

There are numerous indigenous methods of resolving problems in African communities, which are rooted in the cultural and traditional totems of different societies.[42] In African societies, dispute resolution has taken the shape of negotiation, reconciliation, adjudication, and arbitration by seniors.[43] The said methods are not used in a formalised way in traditional communities like in the formalised Western form.[44] Ntuli points out that they have always existed in traditional African communities.[45] Other traditional ways of resolving disputes in indigenous communities are, for

[34] Oguntomisin (2004), p. 11.
[35] Barrett and Barrett (2004), p. 28.
[36] Aiyedun and Ordor (2016), pp. 154–173.
[37] Abe and Ouma (2017), pp. 6–17.
[38] Boniface (2012), p. 391.
[39] Poku (1998), p. 52.
[40] Ghebretekle and Rammala (2018a), p. 331.
[41] Bujo (1998), pp. 198–202.
[42] Rautenbach (2014), p. 290.
[43] Osi (2008b), p. 164.
[44] Spinks (2001), p. 1.
[45] Ntuli (2018), pp. 22–37.

instance, the Traditional Courts in South Africa.[46] The Process circles are also used in customary dispute settlement in African communities.[47] All the afore-stated methods are old techniques of resolving disputes in African traditional communities with the objective to restore the social order, peace and harmony.[48] The Gacaca court in Rwanda is a flagship model for demonstrating that indigenous problem- solving methods can be used in modern day African society to promote reconciliation, restoration, peace and harmony.[49]

In mediation, the process is facilitated by unbiased third parties who assist the parties to reach a mutually acceptable solution. This method has been hailed as very significant to the indigenous communities as it allows the disputants to engage and find their own solution that is reconciliatory.[50] The facilitators are identified from the traditional communities and are mostly elders who are respected for the knowledge and credence they possess in interpreting community problems with the view to resolving them in the best interest of the community.[51] The seniority of the elders and how they master the customs make them very dependable in the activities of traditional communities, particularly when it comes to indigenous problem-solving methods. Once peaceful settlement, reconciliation and forgiveness are reached, the elders would have discharged their duty to promote peace and stability in the village. This method repairs relationships and opens avenues for healing. The contribution by elders has made community life bearable.[52]

Reconciliation takes the form of persuasion by elders or family members to the disputing parties to end their impasse for restoration of peace and harmony.[53] The reconciliatory role is conducted by a person of authority that facilitates dialogue between disputants but is empowered to issue mandatory verdicts to ensure reconciliation and healing.[54] In traditional communities, after settlement is reached, there is normally a celebration through the slaughter of a beast as a form of thanksgiving to the ancestors for spiritually guiding the process, while in other traditional communities the slaughter is used for cleansing, when offences like murder have been committed to allow the dead to rest in peace.[55]

Negotiation in traditional communities is aimed at balancing the interests of the disputants.[56] This is the case also when the community member has offended against the community, the emphasis is on revival of the culprit and reintegration back into

[46] Rautenbach (2015), p. 275.
[47] Daicoff (2015), pp. 427–438.
[48] Omeje (2008), p. 88.
[49] Raper (2005), pp. 1–56.
[50] Chapman and Kagaha (2009), p. 3.
[51] Ghebretekle and Rammala (2018b), p. 336.
[52] Abe (2017), p. 56.
[53] Nhlapo (2005), p. 3.
[54] Ingelare (2008), p. 33.
[55] Umunadi (2011), pp. 64–73.
[56] Muigua (2012), pp. 2–21.

the community.[57] In the traditional Yoruba community in Nigeria, apology for wrongdoing against fellow individual citizens and the entire village was a feature of negotiation.[58] In some instances, fines and compensation were issued, not as punishment but as a form of response to show remorse for the wrongs committed.[59]

Rammala reflects on Lekgotla as another traditional means of resolving disputes used by the traditional community of Makapanstad in the Northwest Province of South Africa.[60] He posits that elders and other respected members of the community of Makapanstad will convene to discuss contentious issues just like other African communities.[61] The significant feature of Lekgotla is its participative nature and the use of idiomatic expression by the elders during the deliberations in trying to find solutions that are mutually beneficial to the community as a collective.[62] Rammala argues that many scholars focus on the outcome of the deliberations, ignoring the rich content provided in the use of idiomatic expression.[63] The close attention on the idiomatic expressions used during Lekgotla shows that they are deeply rooted in the African traditions of Ubuntu and have massive persuasive value toward finding solutions that encourage families to reconciliation and healing.[64] There are preserved social ties and networks that bind the traditional community of Makapanstad together and make it flourish.[65] Lekgotla, as with other traditional conflict methods, allowed the culprits to make confessions in showing that they are remorseful so that apology and request for forgiveness becomes genuine in the eyes of the victims who will be persuaded to accept and forgive.[66] The thematic posture of all idiomatic expressions used at Lekgotla display a strong cultural heritage to build a peaceful and coherent society.[67] The African value of ubuntu, which is the essence of humanity, permeates all the processes of Lekgotla and that explains Lekgotla 's approach of reconciliation and healing. Rautenbach posits that there is a direct correlation between ubuntu and restorative justice.[68] However, Lekgotla has its shortcomings, such as gender bias due to the hierarchies that consider men only, out of touch with reality and the fast pace of modern- day change driven by technology and not appealing to the younger generations.[69] The modern- day complexity of disputes such as insurgency and armed conflicts may be beyond the

[57] Albert et al. (1995), p. 9.

[58] Olaoba (2005), pp. 220–221.

[59] Kariuki (2015), p. 16.

[60] Rammala (2021), pp. 219–241.

[61] Caffery and Mundy (1997), pp. 251–267.

[62] Stipanovich (2017), pp. 513–550.

[63] Rammala (2021), pp. 219–241.

[64] Masina (2000), p. 181.

[65] Etzioni (1996), pp. 1–11.

[66] Rettig (2008a), p. 33.

[67] Cappelletti and Garth (1978), pp. 268–270.

[68] Rautenbach (2015), p. 279.

[69] Bennett (2012), pp. 21–29.

capacity of Lekgotla elders to facilitate a peaceful settlement and ensure justice to the victims.[70] Overall, Lekgotla still remains an integral part of many traditional communities, providing a medium for engagement, dispute resolution and the promotion of peace and harmony in African communities.[71]

In other jurisdictions, the process circle is used where all family members come together and sit in a circle as equals, to discuss family problems that are confronting them like gender- based violence.[72] This form of traditional dispute resolution method was introduced to address family disputes in Cook County Parentage and child support, North America, to address escalating family conflicts.[73] It is interesting to see that the African value of ubuntu features prominently in the circle process and the main theme is that when you hurt another person, you are hurting yourself because we are many but one.[74] The circle's dispute resolution focuses on restorative justice as opposed to retribution.[75] The conversation is facilitated by a reputable member of the family assisted by qualified professionals to ensure that the intended objectives are achieved.[76] This process allows for a non-judgmental conducive space to be created so that the parties involved can feel free to express their feelings and emotions.[77] The perpetrator will express feelings of regret and show remorse for their actions.[78] In family disputes, emotional and spiritual recovery is desirable to allow for reconnection.[79] This approach has helped to reduce gender-based violence and lauded as transformative for the development of the legal system.[80] The restorative approach has also been used to resolve students' sexual related conflicts at universities.[81] It has also assisted certain communities to reduce the level of juvenile incarcerations but instead allowed them to start afresh and reconstruct their lives.[82] Process circles offer an impactful means of resolving disputes in traditional communities and bring peace and harmony in families.[83] Stable families lead to peaceful and cohesive communities.[84] By fostering discussion, respect, and mutual understanding, they can assist to construct communities that are solid and peaceful.

---

[70] Bahtu (2014), p. 109.

[71] Ntuli (2018), p. 56.

[72] Daicoff (2015), pp. 427–438.

[73] Brown (1999), p. 297.

[74] Boniface (2012), p. 378.

[75] Bernard (1996), p. 578.

[76] Gretchen (1999), p. 419.

[77] Bradford (2000a), p. 551.

[78] Van Ness (1997), p. 436.

[79] Goldberg (1997), p. 1003.

[80] Menkel-Meadow (2014), p. 632.

[81] Orcutt (2020), p. 204.

[82] Lyon (2006), pp. 211–248.

[83] Harring (1989), p. 191.

[84] Okulski (2016), pp. 264–307.

4.4 The Gacaca Courts in Rwanda

Abe and Ouma provide a reflection leading to the adoption of customary gacaca courts in Rwanda's formal justice system.[85] After the 1994 massacre which claimed an estimated lives of about 800,000 people over a 100 days, mainly the Tutsis, the Rwandan Judiciary lacked depth to deal with the genocide aftermath to ensure that justice for the victims was seen to be served.[86] This was largely due to the fact that capable and qualified professionals had sought refuge in foreign land.[87] The 1999 Rwandan Truth and Reconciliation Commission recommended the adoption of the traditional gacaca to deal with the offences relating to the genocide.[88] The gacaca institutions were established at lower levels of various Rwandan communities to eradicate a culture of impunity.[89] The gacaca institutions were mandated to find the truth, bring the people of Rwanda together and to hold the culprits accountable.[90] The gacaca courts were designed and accorded full legal authority to address the enormous backlog of cases resulting from the genocide, and to promote truth, justice, and reconciliation in Rwandan communities.[91] The gacaca courts could issue summons, order appearance before it and conduct search and seizure of assets and impose sentences, including life imprisonment.[92] The traditional gacaca, "justice under the tree" portrayed the manner in which the elders conducted it, where they would listen to the issues and discuss while sitting under the tree.[93] The gacaca institution had two components, namely, the reconciliation part as well as the adversarial prosecution part.[94] The reconciliation component allowed interchanges of confessions for indemnity while the other part allowed for prosecution of the more serious offences through a western style formal court proceeding.[95] The restorative posture of gacaca did not inhibit the granting of more severe punishment to the human rights violators as the genocide offences were classified according to the seriousness of participation in genocide atrocities.[96] The apportionment of the sanctions differed depending on whether people participated as orchestrators, heads, assassins, and or demonstrators who damaged houses.[97]

---

[85] Abe and Ouma (2017), pp. 6–7.

[86] Raper (2005), p. 30.

[87] Rawson (2012), p. 115.

[88] Longman (2009), p. 306.

[89] Clark (2010), p. 36.

[90] Chakravarty (1976), p. 91.

[91] Raper (2005), p. 30.

[92] Haberstock (2014), p. 1.

[93] Sarkin (2000), pp. 112–121.

[94] Brounéus (2008), p. 55.

[95] Rettig (2008b), p. 29.

[96] Sullo (2018), p 3.

[97] Briggs and Booth (2001), pp. 9–10.

While there were dissatisfactions amongst communities about gacaca's capacity to ensure the perpetrators of the genocide accounts for their actions, the awareness and educational campaigns bore fruits as people's confidence in gacaca increased.[98] The perpetrators of genocide who confessed to their deeds were rewarded with reduced sentences. The progress made by gacaca assured the Rwandan communities that justice will be served and that the culture of impunity will meet the full might of the law.[99] The expression of public confidence in the gacaca process is demonstrated by the increased number of citizens who use the process.[100] Dispute resolution that is efficient and effective brings healing in African societies.[101] Failure to resolve conflict over limited resources may inhibit reconciliation and degenerate into genocide.[102]

Ghana also had a positive development when its customary problem-solving mechanism was included in the national regulatory framework.[103] The legal system in Ghana, like many African communities, is pluralistic as it includes customary law and common law.[104] The people staying in far flung areas where transportation to formal court locations is a challenge, may benefit from the incorporation of customary law into mainstream legal system to resolve their disputes through mediation, helped by chiefs, headmen, family members, and community leaders who know how to interpret communal values to bring about reconciliation, peace and harmony to ensure stable society.[105]

Kenyan law made it a requirement that both ADR and indigenous dispute resolution methods must be used before litigation.[106] This has brought about more accessibility to the justice system.[107] When everyone is able to make use of the Justice system, the rule of law and stability gain prominence.[108] Muigua and Francis posit that resolution of disputes making use of the justice system contributes to advancement of life.[109] In Kenya, the application of TDRMs to conflict will enhance access to justice.[110] The inclusion of customary law in the formal justice settings will contribute to development in Kenya given the communal values that promote peace and harmony in the community which is a viable environment for growth.[111] The

[98] Dumas (2020), pp. 133–143.
[99] Daly (2002), p. 363.
[100] Clamp (2013), p. 17.
[101] Minow (1988), p. 15
[102] Kerr and Mobekk (2007), p. 154.
[103] Uwazie (2011), pp. 1–6.
[104] Alternative Dispute Resolution Act 798 of 2010.
[105] CONSTITUTION OF THE REPUBLIC OF GHANA, 1992.
[106] Article 159 of the Constitution.
[107] Kinama (2015), p. 22.
[108] Justin (2021), pp. 61–72.
[109] Muigua and Francis (2015), p. 1.
[110] Kariuki (2014), pp. 202–228.
[111] Owens and Shaw (1984), p. 3.

ADR and TDRMs enhance developmental goals by providing easy access to justice for the poor.[112] There is a link between the rule of law and advancement of the peoples' needs.[113] The increased use of the justice system, as improved by the option of traditional dispute resolution methods in Kenya, contributes to the strengthening of the rule of law.[114]

Ethiopia's justice system also had a fabric of legal pluralism.[115] The traditional dispute resolution method adopted a religious posture due to the influence of Christianity, Judaism and Islam religions.[116] The communities living in the Western Ethiopia adopted *Michu,* a concept denoting friendship method of dispute resolution, translated to mean living side by side in peace and harmony.[117] This method was preferred because of many immigrants in the area and the inhabitants of the area extended a warm welcome to them.[118] *Michu*'s slogan was pivotal like Ubuntu in South Africa when handling disputes that related to land territory, grazing fields boundaries and inter-marriages.[119] Intervention by the authorities was not desirable as the formal justice system passed judgement instead of restoring relations.[120]

In all the traditional problem- solving methods, council of the elders is at the centre.[121] Kenyatta posits that the role and responsibility of the senior towards both his family as well as his village, is to bring harmony to the work of the different groups, including those who are still alive as well as the deceased.[122] The elder is respected for his superiority and prudence whilst he reveres the supremacy of the ancestral soul.[123]

4.5 Benefits, Shortcomings, Challenges and Recommendations

There are identifiable benefits to be derived from the traditional dispute resolution methods as there are disadvantages.[124] These methods are embedded in cultural practices and traditions, hence they withstood the test of time when they were pushed

[112] Michel (2011), p. 1.
[113] Rukwaro (1994), p. 1.
[114] Muigua and Francis (2015), pp. 1–11.
[115] Kariuki (2015), p. 9.
[116] Bahtu (2014), p. 109.
[117] Myers and Shinn (2010), p. 7.
[118] Kariuki (2015), p. 9.
[119] Kariuki (2015), p. 9.
[120] Umunadi (2011), pp. 64–73.
[121] Kazeem (2009), pp. 60–67.
[122] Kenyatta (1965), pp. 38–41.
[123] Muigua (2018), pp. 84–168.
[124] Okulski (2016), pp. 264–307.

aside by colonial rulers.[125] The indigenous problem- solving methods are restorative and less adversarial in nature and their focus is on truth, reconciliation and healing.[126] These methods thrive on involvement by the community and adherence to cultural practices and traditions, which make it difficult for anyone not to comply with the orders issued by the council of elders.[127] Ntuli observed that many Africans are inhibited from participating in formal justice processes due to a number of factors, for instance, travelling distance and cost, the protracted proceedings, the unfamiliar languages used as well as the methods employed to conduct the proceedings in formal courts.[128] The traditional methods enable access by rural communities to justice as they are located within the communities where they live. Accordingly, access to justice advances development.[129] Aiyedun and Odor acclaim the customary methods for being simple, flexible, informal and cost effective as opposed to the formal justice system that uses complex methods of proof and decision.[130] Most scholars argue that these methods offer a win-win situation as opposed to litigation that is costly and unbearable, have long delays and complex processes, and that they make the poor feel excluded, discriminated against and marginalised.[131]

The disadvantage regarding the indigenous methods of dispute resolution is that in many communities, they have not been institutionalised into regulatory frameworks.[132] In most African countries which have a pluralistic justice system, the traditional methods have gained recognition in the national laws and largely used by traditional communities.[133] Institutions like Lekgotla may find that compliance with their decisions is only voluntary and has no enforcement mechanism except for the collective pressure from the community.[134] The council of the elders may not possess the skill to deal with complex cases that may need the support of modern day technology.[135]

There are also a number of challenges regarding traditional dispute resolution methods.[136] The indigenous methods often get defiance from civilised Africans.[137] Customary justice systems are given inferior status as opposed to the formal western

[125]Huston (2015), p. 218.

[126]Murithi (2006), pp. 30–32.

[127]Pieterse (2001), pp. 364–377.

[128]Ntuli (2018), pp. 22–37.

[129]Spinks (2001).

[130]Aiyedun and Ordor (2016), pp. 154–173.

[131]Mamdani (1966), p. 118.

[132]Ibe and Abugu (2022b), pp. 11–45.

[133]South African Law Commission (SALC) Project 90 Customary Law "Report on Traditional courts and the Judicial function of traditional leaders (2003) 1.

[134]Rammala (2021), pp. 219–241.

[135]Ntuli (2018), pp. 22–37.

[136]Bowd (2009).

[137]Bradford (2000b), p. 582.

justice system.[138] The traditional justice system is susceptible to fraud and corruption as the elders are not paid to resolve disputes for traditional communities.[139] In addition, there has been a breakdown of the social ties that bounded the communities together as cohesive units.[140] The elders are no longer commanding the respect and influence they used to as in the olden days. The lack of appeal options against decisions of the elders may discourage people from participating.[141]

The proposal is made that traditional dispute resolution methods, as well as ADR methods, be institutionalised as part of the formal justice system.[142] The role of the elders needs to be amplified through training and compensation to prevent corruption risk.[143] There must be integration of customary problem- solving methods and Western ADR, complemented by the use of technology in African communities.[144]

4.6 Conclusion

The indigenous problem solving methods have demonstrated a high level of resilience amid Western formal justice bullying.[145] The traditional methods proved to be more efficient and impactful in fostering peace, harmony and stability in rural communities. However, more development is required to ensure that the customary methods are strengthened through education and compensation for the elders given their. Prominent role. There is a need for integration of the traditional problem solving methods and modern ADR processes into the regulatory framework of African communities.

References

Abe O (2017) Conflict resolution in the extractives: a consideration of traditional conflict resolution paradigms in post-colonial Africa. Willamette J Int Law Disput Resolut 25(1):56

Abe E, Ouma S (2017) A re-assessment of the impact and potency of traditional dispute resolution mechanism in post- conflict Africa. Ave Maria Int Law J 6:1

Abifarin O et al (2019) Dispute resolution within/between religious Organisations in Nigeria: litigation or alternative dispute resolution? Univ Gambia Law Rev 2:6

[138] Huyse and Salter (2008).

[139] Spinks (2001).

[140] Aiyedun and Ononogbu (2015), p. 77.

[141] Kariuki (2018), p. 37.

[142] Tesfay and Tafere (2004).

[143] Wojkowska (2006), pp. 20–24.

[144] South African Law Commission. (1999). Project 90: The Harmonisation of Common Law and Indigenous Law. Report of Conflicts of Law.

[145] Uwazie (2011), p. 16.

Adefisoye TO, Africa BO (2018) Understanding and managing violent conflicts. Conflict Stud Q 22:3–4
Aiyedun O, Ononogbu I (2015) Transformation of dispute resolution in Africa. IJODR 2:77
Aiyedun A, Ordor A (2016) Integrating the traditional with the contemporary in dispute resolution in Africa. Law Democracy Dev 20:154–173
Ajayi AT, Buhari LO (2014) Methods of conflict resolution in African traditional society. Afr Res Rev 8(2):138
Albert IO, Awe T, Herault G, Omitoogun W (1995) Informal channels for conflict resolution in Ibadan, Nigeria. Institut français de recherche en Afrique, Ibadan, p 9
Annan N (2014) Violent conflicts and civil strife in West Africa: causes, challenges and prospects. Stability Int J Secur Dev 3(1):1
Bahtu GT (2014) Popular dispute resolution mechanisms in Ethiopia: trends, opportunities, challenges and prospects, p 109
Barrett JT, Barrett JA (2004) History of alternative dispute resolution. The story of a political, social and cultural movement Jessey Bass 28
Bennett T (2012) Access to justice and human rights in the traditional courts of sub-Saharan Africa. In: Bennett T et al (eds) African perspectives on tradition and justice. Intersentia, pp 21–29
Bernard PE (1996) Community and conscience: the dynamic challenge of lawyers: ethics in tribal Peacemaking. U TOL Law Rev 27:578
Boniface AE (2012) African-style mediation and Western-style divorce and family mediation: reflections for the south African context. Potchefstroom Electronic Law J 15(5):378
Bosman L, Kimani S (2018) Approaches to investor state dispute resolution in eastern Africa: Rwanda, Kenya and Mauritius. Acta Jurídica:113–148
Bowd R (2009) Access to justice in Africa: comparison between Sierra Leone, Tanzania and Zambia. [policy brief]. Institute for Security Studies, Pretoria
Bradford WC (2000a) Reclaiming indigenous legal autonomy on the path to peaceful coexistence: the theory, practice, and limitations of tribal peacemaking in Indian dispute resolution. North Dakota Law Rev 76(3):551
Bradford WC (2000b) Reclaiming indigenous legal autonomy on the path to peaceful coexistence: the theory, practice, and limitations of tribal peacemaking in Indian dispute resolution. North Dakota Law Rev 76(3):582
Briggs P, Booth J (2001) Rwanda: the Bradt travel guide, pp 9–10
Brounéus K (2008) Truth-telling as talking cure? Insecurity and Retraumatization in the Rwandan Gacaca courts. Secur Dialogue 39(1):55
Brown HL (1999) The Navajo Nation's peacemaker division: an integrated, Community-based dispute resolution Forum. Am Indian Law Rev 24(2):297
Bujo B (1988) The ethical dimension of Community-the African model and the dialogue between north and south. Pauline's Publications Africa, pp 198–202
Bujo B (1998) The ethical dimension of community- the African model and the dialogue between north and south. Pauline Publication, Johannesburg, p 198
Caffery S, Mundy G (1997) Informal Systems of Justice: the formation of law within gypsy communities. Am J Comp Law 45(2):251–267
Cappelletti M, Garth B (1978) Access to justice: the worldwide movement to make rights effective, a general report. In: Cappelletti M, Garth B (eds) Access to justice: a world survey, vol 1. Giuffre Editore, Milan, pp 268–270
Chakravarty A (1976) Investing in authoritarian rule: punishment and patronage in Rwanda's Gacaca courts for genocide crimes. Cambridge University Press, Cambridge [UK]; New York, p 91
Chapman C, Kagaha A (2009) Resolving disputes using traditional mechanisms in the Karamoja and Teso regions of Uganda. Minor Rights Int 2009:3
Clamp K (2013) Restorative justice in transition, vol 17. Routledge
Clark P (2010) The Gacaca courts, post-genocide justice and reconciliation in Rwanda: justice without lawyers. Cambridge University Press, New York, p 36

Daicoff SS (2015) Families in circle process: restorative justice in family law. Fam Court Rev 53(3): 427

Daly E (2002) Between punitive and reconstructive justice: the Gacaca courts in Rwanda. New York Univ J Int Law Politics 34:363

Dieng A (2011) ADR in Sub-Saharan African Countries (Arbitration, Mediation and Conciliation Centre of Dakar) 1

Dumas H (2020) Judging neighbours: the gacaca courts in Rwanda. South Central Rev:133–143

Edzii JE (2018) Is alternative dispute resolution a solution to interpersonal and group conflicts in West Africa? The case of Ghana (a Masters' dissertation submitted to the Faculty of law, University of Ghana, Legon,) 46

Etzioni A (1996) The responsive community. Am Sociol Rev 61(1):1

ISS REPORT (2017) African Conflicts to watch in 2022. *ISS AFRICA* 1

Ghebretekle TB, Rammala M (2018a) Traditional African conflict resolution: the case of South Africa and Ethiopia. Mizan Law Rev 12(2):325–347

Ghebretekle TB, Rammala M (2018b) Traditional African conflict resolution: the case of South Africa and Ethiopia. Mizan Law Rev 12(2):336

Goldberg CE (1997) Overextended borrowing: tribal Peacemaking applied in non-Indian disputes. Wash L Rev 72:1003

Gretchen U (1999) Widening the circle: adapting traditional Indian dispute resolution methods to implement alternative dispute resolution and restorative justice in modern communities. Hamline J Public Law Policy 20(2):419

Haberstock L (2014) An analysis of the effectiveness of the Gacaca court system in post-genocide Rwanda. Global Tides 1

Harring SL (1989) Crow Dog's case: a chapter in the legal history of tribal sovereignty. Am Indian Law Rev 14:191

Home R (2020) Land dispute resolution and the right to development in Africa. Journal Juridical Sci 45(1):72–92

Huston CM (2015) Restorative justice: a comparative analysis of campus implementation, vol 218. Honors College

Huyse L, Salter M (2008) Traditional justice and reconciliation after violent conflict. Learning from African experiences. International Institute for Democracy and Electoral Assistance, Stockholm

Ibe E, Abugu U (2022a) Issues and challenges of promoting excellence in alternative dispute resolution in Africa. Int J Legis Drafting Law Reform 11:36–49

Ibe E, Abugu U (2022b) Issues and challenges of promoting excellence in alternative dispute resolution in Africa. Int J Legisl Draft Law Reform 11:45

Ingelare B (2008) The Gacaca courts in Rwanda. Traditional justice and conflict resolution after violent conflict: learning from African experiences, Luc Huyse and mark Salter (Eds) IDEA, Stockholm, 33

Kariuki F (2014) Applicability of traditional dispute resolution mechanisms in criminal cases in Kenya: Case study of Repulic i' Mohamed Abdon Mohamed [2013] eKLR,' 2 Altern Disput Resolut J 202–228

Kariuki F (2015) Conflict resolution by elders in Africa: successes, challenges and opportunities. Chartered Institute of Arbitrators Conference, 2015

Kazeem FA (2009) Agba (elder) as arbitrator: a Yoruba socio-political model for conflict resolution-a Review of Lawrence O. Bamikole. J Law Confl Resolut 1(3):60–67

Kenyatta J (1965) Facing mount Kenya: the tribal life of the Gikuyu. 38

Kerr R, Mobekk E (2007) Peace and justice: seeking accountability after war. Polity Press, p 154

Kinama E (2015) Traditional justice systems as alternative dispute resolution under article 159(2) (c) of the constitution of Kenya, 2010. Strathmore Law J 1:22

Longman T (2009) An assessment of Rwanda's Gacaca courts. Peace Rev: J Soc Just 21(3):306

Lyon CE (2006) Alternative methods for sentencing youthful offenders: using traditional tribal methods as model. Ave Maria Law Rev 4(1):211

Mamdani M (1966) Citizen and subject: contemporary Africa and the legacy of late colonialism. Princeton University Press, p 118
Mandova E (2013) The Shona proverb as an expression of unhu/Ubuntu. Int J Acad Res Prog Educ Dev 2(1):100–108
Masina N (2000) Xhosa practices of Ubuntu for South Africa. In: Zartman W (ed) Traditional cures for modern conflicts: African conflict medicine, p 181
Menkel-Meadow C (2014) Unsettling the lawyers: other forms of justice in indigenous claims of expropriation, abuse, and injustice. Univ Toronto Law J 64:632
Michel J (2011) Alternative dispute resolution and the rule of law in international development cooperation. Justice & Development Working Paper Series,1
Minow M (1988) Between vengeance and forgiveness, vol 15. Beacon Press
Muigua K (2012) Resolving conflicts through mediation in Kenya, vol 2. Glenwood Publishers Ltd, Nairobi, p 21
Muigua K (2018) Institutionalising traditional dispute resolution mechanisms and other Community justice systems. Altern Disput Resolut 6(1):84–168
Muigua K, Francis K (2015) Alternative dispute resolution: access to justice and development in Kenya. Strathmore Law J 1:1
Murithi T (2006) Practical peacemaking wisdom from Africa: reflections on Ubuntu. J Pan Afr Stud 1(4):30–32
Myers LJ, Shinn DH (2010) Appreciating traditional forms of healing conflict and in Africa and the world. Black Diaspora Rev 2(1):7
Nhlapo T (2005) The judicial function of traditional leaders: a contribution to restorative justice? Paper presented at the Conference of the Association of Law Reform Agencies of Eastern and Southern Africa Cape Town, 3
Ntuli N (2018) Alternative dispute resolution in a comparative perspective. Conflict Stud Q 22:37
Oguntomisin GO (2004) The process of peacekeeping and peace-making in pre-colonial Nigeria. John Achers, Ibadan, p 11
Okonkwo T (2017) Maritime boundaries delimitation and dispute resolution in Africa. Beijing Law Rev 8:55
Okulski JE (2016) Complex adaptive peacemaking. How systems theory reveals advantages of traditional tribal dispute resolution methods. Am Indian Law J 5:264
Olaoba OB (2001) An introduction to Africa legal culture 1
Olaoba O (2005) Ancestral focus and the process of conflict resolution in traditional African societies. In: Albert AO (ed) Perspectives on peace and conflict in Africa in essays in honour of general (Dr) Abdul Salam a, Abubakar. John Achers Ltd., Ibadan, pp 220–221
Olaoba OB (2010) African Traditional Methods of Conflict Resolution. PCR831: Course Guide, 25 (NOUN, Lagos)
Oluduro O (2011) Customary arbitration in Nigeria: development and prospects. Afr J Int Comp Law 19(2):307
Omeje KC (2008) Understanding conflict resolution in Africa. In: Francis DJ (ed) Peace and conflict in Africa. Zed Books, London, p 88
Onigun O, Albert IO (eds) (2001) Community conflicts in Nigeria, management, resolution and transformation. Spectrum Books Limited, Ibadan, Nigeria
Orcutt M et al (2020) Restorative justice approaches to the informal resolution of student sexual misconduct. JC Univ Law 45:204
Osi O (2008a) Understanding indigenous dispute resolution processes and Western alternative dispute resolution, cultivating culturally appropriate methods in lieu of litigation. Cardozo J Conflict Resolut 10(1):163
Osi O (2008b) Understanding indigenous dispute resolution processes and Western alternative dispute resolution, cultivating culturally appropriate methods in lieu of litigation. Cardozo J Conflict Resolut 10(1):164
Owens E, Shaw R (1984) Development reconsidered: bridging the gap between government and the people, vol 3. Lexington Books

Pieterse M (2001) It's a black thing: upholding culture and customary law in a society founded on non-racialism. SAJHR 17:364–377

Pimentel D (2011) Legal pluralism in post-colonial Africa: linking statutory and customary adjudication in Mozambique. Yale Hum Rights Dev J 14(59):3

Pkalya R, Adan M, Masinde I (2004) Indigenous democracy: traditional conflict reconciliation mechanisms among the Pokot, Turkana, Samburu and the Marakwet. In: Rabar B, Kirimi M (eds) Intermediate technology development group-eastern Africa, pp 89–95

Poku H (1998) African ethnicity; history, conflict management, resolution and prevention. University Press of America, Inc, p 52

Price E (2018) Alternative dispute resolution in Africa: is ADR the bridge between traditional and modern dispute resolution. Pepperdine Dispute Resol Law J 18(3):1

Rammala MRN (2021) Lekgotla and idiomatic expressions in traditional dispute resolution: the case of Makapanstad, north-West Province. South Africa' Int J Afr Renaissance Stud 219

Raper J (2005) The gacaca experiment: Rwanda's restorative dispute resolution response to the 1994 genocide. Pepperdine Dispute Resol Law J 5(1):1

Rautenbach C (2014) Traditional courts as alternative dispute resolution (ADR)-mechanisms in South Africa. SSRN 290

Rautenbach C (2015) Legal reform of traditional courts in South Africa: exploring the links between Ubuntu, restorative justice and therapeutic jurisprudence. J Int Comp Law 2(2):275

Rawson D (2012) From retribution to reconciliation: transitional justice in Rwanda,1994-2011. Georgetown J Int Aff 13(2):115

Rettig M (2008a) Gacaca: truth, justice, and reconciliation in post-conflict Rwanda? Afr Stud Rev 51(3):33

Rettig M (2008b) Gacaca: truth, justice, and reconciliation in post conflict Rwanda? Afr Stud Rev 29

Rukwaro GK (1994) The rule of law and development. In: Vyas Y et al (eds) Law and development in the third world. University of Nairobi, p 1

Sarkin J (2000) Promoting justice, truth and reconciliation in transitional societies: evaluating Rwanda's approach in the new millennium of using Community based Gacaca tribunals to Deal with the past. Int Law FORUM Du Droit Int 2:112–121

Spinks M (2001) Access to justice in sub-Saharan Africa: the role of tradition and informal justice systems, vol 1. Penal Reform International

Stipanovich TJ (2017) Living the dream of ADR: reflections on four decades of the quiet revolution in dispute resolution. Cardozo J Confl Resolut 18(3):513–550

Sullo P (2018) Beyond genocide: transitional justice and gacaca courts in Rwanda, the search for truth, justice and reconciliation. Asser Press, Heidelberger Platz. Berlin, Germany 51(3): 3

Tesfay Y, Tafere K (2004) Indigenous rangeland resources and conflict management by the North Afar pastoral groups in Ethiopia. Drylands Coordination Group (DCG), Oslo

Umunadi KE (2011a) The efficiency of mediation and negotiation methods for dispute resolution in Delta state. Sacha J Policy Strateg Stud 1(2):64–73

Uwazie EE (2011) Alternative dispute resolution in Africa: preventing conflict and enhancing stability. African Security Brief, pp 1–6

Van der Waal CS (2006) Formal and informal dispute resolution. In: Hinz MO, Pateman K (eds) The shade of new leaves: governance in traditional authority: a southern African perspective. LIT Verlag, Munster, p 140

Van Ness DW (1997) Perspectives on achieving satisfying justice: values and principles of restorative justice. Int'l Community Corrections 20(8):436

Wojkowska E (2006) Doing justice: how informal justice systems can contribute. UNDP, Oslo, pp 20–24

Mr. Matome Malatsi was born on 22 January 1966. He holds M Phil (Workplace Ethics) from the University of Pretoria (2012). He obtained B. Juris and LLB degrees from the University of Venda in 1989 and 1994 respectively. He is an admitted attorney of the High Court of South Africa (2000). He is a certified Ethics Officer conferred by the University of Stellenbosch and the Ethics Institute of South Africa. Mr. Malatsi has Specialist training in Advanced Law Enforcement Management with International Law Enforcement Academy in Roswell, USA (2003). He also undertook a special training in Investigation of Organized Crime at the Federal Bureau of Investigations (FBI) US Department of Justice, Quantico, Virginia, USA (2000). Mr. Malatsi joined government in November 2000, starting at the NPA's Directorate of Special Operations (DSO), commonly known as the Scorpions. His roles included but not limited to investigation of priority organised crime in South Africa as well as handling misconduct cases of both investigators and prosecutors. On 1 March 2004, he joined the Department of Correctional Services as Director: Departmental Investigation Unit where he successfully set up a capacity to prevent and combat contraband, fraud, and corruption in the department. On 01 February 2013, he joined the Department of Home Affairs as Chief Director: Investigations where he introduced mechanisms to combat Identity document fraud and corruption as well as the Ethics Management program. On 01 October 2017, he was appointed by the Public Service Commission (PSC) as the Deputy Director General: Integrity and Anti- Corruption (DDG:IAC), overseeing the implementation of Ethics framework and Anti- corruption policies in the Public Service and administration of South Africa, the role which includes, inter alia, dispute resolution in the workplace, rapid response on service delivery interventions, promotion of professional ethics, mitigation of Conflicts of interest through Financial Disclosure Framework and the investigation of complaints in respect to public administration and personnel practices i.e. appointments and supply chain management irregularities. He is registered for LLM: Alternative Dispute Resolution at the University of Pretoria (2023).

Chapter 5
The Role of Mediation in Land Disputes in Africa

Mmakgoedi Rakgwale

5.1 Introduction

Land is a natural resource valued by humans. The scarcity of land leads to disputes. In order to address the apartheid legacy of land dispossession the South African Constitution[1] provides for restitution and land tenure.[2] This chapter will provide an overview of mediation as a dispute resolution mechanism. The key concepts and principles of mediation are discussed. The relevance of mediation in land dispute resolution is important in the resolution of disputes. Factors that play a pivotal role are cultural and contextual factors influencing mediation in land disputes. This chapter will provide a comparative analysis of mediation processes and practices used in South Africa, Kenya and Rwanda. There will be an examination of the roles and qualifications for mediators in each country.

5.2 Overview of Mediation

Mediation can be said to be a voluntary yet confidential dispute resolution process.[3] It involves a third party referred to as a mediator who aids parties in conflict to reach a mutually acceptable resolution.[4] Mediation is quite different from litigation as it

This chapter is based on the Chapter 1 of the LLM mini dissertation of the author M Rakgwale, which available on the UP Law repository website.

[1] The Constitution of the Republic of South Africa (1996).

[2] Final Report of the Presidential Advisory Panel on Land Reform and Agriculture 2019.

[3] Andrew (2003), pp. 117–130.

[4] Andrew (2003), pp. 117–130.

R. Baboolal Frank (ed.), *Dispute Resolution within Africa*,
https://doi.org/10.1007/978-3-031-76261-1_5

encourages parties to have open communication and collaboration.[5] This process involves the mediator facilitating discussions in order to identify issues that help get to resolution options.[6] Mediation has been used in a lot of contexts, from family disputes to business disagreements and now also used for land disputes.[7] Mediation has brought benefits some of which include cost-effectiveness, preservation of relationships and quicker resolution, making it gain more traction as opposed to litigation.

5.3 Mediator's Role

Mediator's role is to guide the whole process in order to ensure fairness and respect. His/her duty is not to impose decisions but rather assist parties in exploring options and finding a common ground.[8] Mediation can therefore be said to be important as it encourages collaborative problem-solving while preserving relationships.[9] At most times it results in agreements that all parties find acceptable ensuring sustainable resolution.

5.4 Principles of Mediation

There are core principles of mediation that ensure a dispute is successfully resolved.

Mediation requires that parties engage freely, ensuring their active involvement and commitment to resolutions.[10] It provides for informed consent which involves understanding the mediation process and its implications.[11] Impartiality and neutrality is also important. This means mediators should remain unbiased and neutral in order to ensure a balanced approach that involves all parties.[12] The avoidance of favouritism ensures trust and confidence from disputing parties.[13] Confidentiality is another principle; mediation discussions are private and confidential to ensure open communication.[14] There may be exceptions in instances where threats of harm are

[5]MacDonnell (1988), pp. 1–19.
[6]MacDonnell (1988), pp. 1–19.
[7]Bourdier (2019), pp. 55–76.
[8]Boulle and Rycroft (1998), p. 167.
[9]Boulle and Rycroft (1998), p. 167.
[10]Octaleny et al. (2020), pp. 21–39.
[11]Octaleny et al. (2020), p. 21–39.
[12]Derevyanko et al. (2023), pp. 248–256.
[13]Derevyanko et al. (2023), pp. 248–256.
[14]Caser et al. (2017), p. 109120.

clearly stated to maintain trust while ensuring safety.[15] Parties Self-determination means they have the autonomy to make decisions about the resolution empowering them in the process, this is another principle.[16] Mediators aid this self-discovery and decision-making without imposing their opinions.[17]

5.5 Key Concepts of Mediation Process

The key concepts of the mediation process involve four phases. Firstly there is an opening session, this is where mediators set the tone by explaining the process and ground rules.[18] Parties have the opportunity to discuss the issues at hand, express their concerns and reach an agreement with regards to which topics will be addressed. Then we have the second phase which is the exploration phase. At this point underlying issues are identified in order to understand the root cause of the dispute.[19] It involves clarifying interests, needs and goals for effective communication. The third phase is the negotiation phase. Here there is generation of options and brainstorming creative solution.[20] The mediator facilitates communication between parties so they express their views and explore compromises where necessary.[21] Lastly is the agreement phase, it involves drafting a clear and comprehensive agreement that is a reflection of the parties' decisions.[22] This ensures parties understand the terms fully and are willing to abide by them.[23]

5.6 Relevance of Mediation to Land Disputes

Mediation plays a crucial role in resolving disputes and this has made it relevant to land disputes for several reasons. For starters mediators that are experienced in land disputes bring valuable expertise to the table.[24] They do this by helping parties understand zoning regulations, property laws and all the relevant information to make informed decisions.[25] There are often deep emotional ties to land and property

---

15 Caser et al. (2017), p. 109120.

16 Betts (1999), pp. 161–183.

17 Gren (2016), p. 75.

18 Mckersie et al. (2004), pp. 13–35.

19 Mckersie et al. (2004), pp. 13–35.

20 Antes et al. (1998), p. 287.

21 Lempereur et al. (2021), p. 1–24.

22 Hansen (2003), p. 297.

23 Hansen (2003), p. 297.

24 Shamir (2016), pp. 23–36.

25 Shamir (2016), pp. 23–36.

and mediation provides a supportive platform which enables parties to express their emotions and concerns.[26] The agreements reached through land dispute mediation are most likely to be adhered to because they are mutual.[27] Mediation has also assisted in ensuring parties consider long-term solutions and sustainable land use practices.[28] This is important in disputes related to land development, property boundaries or environmental concerns.[29] Where land disputes involve communities, mediation helps keep harmony and cohesion within the community for a shared resolution.[30] The relevance of mediation to land disputes can therefore be said to be in its ability to offer efficient and cost effective solutions that are customized, preserve relationships and maintain privacy.[31] Mediation is a valuable alternative to litigation and ensures land-related conflicts are resolved in a satisfactory manner.

5.7 Cultural Factors Influencing Mediation in Land Disputes

It's important that we recognise the cultural norms that are crucial for mediation. This allows outcomes that are sensitive to specific needs and values of parties. Cultural norms and values related to land ownership for example, there are different traditional beliefs and customs, and some may regard land as a sacred entity or ancestral heritage.[32] There are also rituals and ceremonies associated with land use that can affect negotiations.[33] Indigenous communities usually have different communal land ownership structures; this means mediators must respect indigenous knowledge and governing systems.[34] Non-verbal cues and communication styles is another example. Gestures and symbols are important as they convey emotions and intentions.[35] Should there be misinterpretation of gestures during mediation, it can lead to misunderstandings.[36] There is also the issue of language barrier and translation issues, this often results in miscommunication and misrepresentation of intentions it's therefore required that there are skilled interpreters during mediation to breach the language and communication gaps.[37] Lastly social hierarchies and power

[26] Jones (2001), pp. 217–244.
[27] Dhiaulhaq et al. (2015), pp. 132–145.
[28] Dhiaulhaq et al. (2015), pp. 132–145.
[29] Yanto (2023), pp. 370–376.
[30] Wehrmann (2008), pp. 1–55.
[31] Andrew (2003), pp. 117–130.
[32] Di (2009), pp. 288–245.
[33] Basita (2001), pp. 1–13.
[34] Zhomartkyzy (2023), p. 230.
[35] Oleksik et al. (2014), pp. 1243–1257.
[36] Oleksik et al. (2014), pp. 1243–1257.
[37] Hertig (2004), pp. 59–72.

dynamics have influence on land mediation.[38] The influence of community leaders and elders often has a great influence on how disputes are resolved.[39] It's important those mediators are able to navigate through the power dynamics with respect and maintain impartiality.[40] Gender roles can also affect participation of women in mediation therefore mediators must ensure gender-inclusive mediation process that addresses the power imbalance.[41]

5.8 Contextual Factors Influencing Mediation in Land Disputes

Contextual factors also play a role in the influence of mediation. Legal frameworks and property rights is one of the factors. The variety of legal systems has an impact on ownership of land because of how it is defined and contested for.[42] Mediators need to be exposed to all the relevant laws in order to provide a platform for informed discussions.[43] The historical injustices and land dispossession have an influence on current disputes.[44] Mediators acknowledging historical context is important for reconciliation-based solutions.[45] The link between economic factors and land value is another context to be considered.[46] Economic disparities can make land conflicts more serious especially in land that is full of resources.[47] Mediators are therefore tasked with finding sustainable solutions that address underlying economic issues.[48] Where there are corporate interest and development projects, there can be displacement and conflict.[49] The need to balance economic development with community rights becomes a challenge for mediators.[50] Political stability and government involvement is another underlying factor that influences mediation of land disputes.[51] There are government policies and interventions that influence land disputes.[52] Mediators are required to understand political dynamics in order to

---

[38] Narain (2019), p. 1607.

[39] Blench et al. (2006), pp. 1–10.

[40] Blench et al. (2006), pp. 1–10.

[41] Allen (2014), pp. 1–14.

[42] Al-Amin and Akter (2022), pp. 4218–4225.

[43] Al-Amin and Akter (2022), pp. 4218–4225.

[44] Gibson (2009), pp. 1–4.

[45] Gibson (2009), pp. 1–25.

[46] Bob (2010), pp. 49–51.

[47] Issaka (2023), pp. 141–152.

[48] Engel and Korf (2005), pp. 1–162.

[49] Girke (2015), pp. 509–524.

[50] Viscidi and Fargo (2015).

[51] Dhiaulhaq et al. (2018), pp. 64–72.

[52] Zhang et al. (2024), pp. 1–3.

control how the government gets involved effectively.[53] Political tensions may also intensify land disputes which then complicates resolution process.[54] It is therefore a requirement that mediators encourage dialogue to minimise political challenges.[55]

5.9 Comparative Analysis of Mediation Processes and Practices Used in South Africa, Kenya and Rwanda

Each country's approach to land dispute mediation is a reflection of its historical, cultural and legal context. South Africa, Kenya and Rwanda provide a diverse context for land dispute mediation.

5.9.1 South Africa

South Africa consists of mediation process that provides for court-annexed mediation.[56] Trained mediators facilitate negotiations between disputing parties. This is often used in urban areas.[57] There is also community-based and traditional leader's mediation.[58] This is often used in rural areas where involvement of community and traditional leaders are important.[59] These leaders play a crucial role in resolving land related disputes. The legal framework for land disputes is the land reform laws. The Land Reform Act provides guidelines for land disputes.[60] There are also specialised land claims courts to handle disputes related to restitution and land rights that encourage mediated settlements.[61] South African approach is focused on addressing historical injustices such as the land dispossession that occurred during apartheid era which makes it unique from other countries due to its emphasis on transformation and restitution.[62] The challenges faced by South Africa include its complex historical context. The history of apartheid-era land dispossession makes land disputes more complicated and requires sensitive, subtle mediation approaches.[63] Communication between formal and traditional systems is another challenge as it is

[53] Nussbaum (2016), p. 361.
[54] Dhiaulhaq et al. (2018), pp. 64–72.
[55] Elliot (1999), pp. 199–240.
[56] Olivier (2018), pp. 1–10.
[57] Olivier (2018), pp. 1–100.
[58] Cousins and Kepe (2004), pp. 41–54.
[59] Cousins and Kepe (2004), pp. 41–54.
[60] The Land Reform Act of 1996, South Africa.
[61] Geldenhuys (2017), pp. 20–24.
[62] Ntsebeza (2007), pp. 1–6.
[63] Ntsebeza (2007), pp. 1–6.

necessary for successful mediation outcomes especially in areas where traditional practices have a huge influence.[64]

5.9.2 *Kenya*

Kenya consists of a mediation process that is formal and informal.[65] There is court based and community based mediation.[66] Informally disputes are resolved by local elders or community leaders governed by traditional customs and practices.[67] The Kenyan judiciary actively promotes alternative dispute resolution mechanisms such as mediation of land disputes.[68] The Kenyan legal framework consist of land acts thus The Land Act[69] and Land Registration Act[70] provides the legal framework for land mediation in Kenya. These laws establish the rights of individual and communities regarding land use and ownership.[71] Kenya also has a small claims court that allows parties to resolve land disputes inexpensively through mediation.[72] The challenge faced by Kenya is the limited access to legal representation for disadvantaged communities which ultimately affects the fairness of mediation process.[73] Mediated agreements may also face challenges related enforcement due to corruption.[74]

5.9.3 *Rwanda*

Rwanda consists of community –based mediation through the "Abunzi" system.[75] Trained mediators at villages handle disputes such as land disputes.[76] This ensures accessibility and cultural relevance.[77] There are also mediation committees established at grassroots level, this promotes local participation and ownership in

[64] Puri et al. (2004), pp. 42–52.
[65] Mtuku et al. (2022), pp. 1–19.
[66] Muigai (2017), pp. 1–7.
[67] Mtuku et al. (2022), pp. 1–19.
[68] Wambua (2013), pp. 15–33.
[69] The Land Act of 2012.
[70] Land Registration Act of 2012.
[71] Alden Wily (2018), p. 12.
[72] Mwaura (2016).
[73] Djurfeldt (2020), p. 104305.
[74] Djurfeldt (2020), p. 104305.
[75] Mutisi (2011), p. 1–5.
[76] Mutisi (2011), pp. 41–47.
[77] Van Hemert (2019), p. 101730.

dispute resolution process.[78] The Rwanda legal framework consists of land law. Rwanda's 2013 Land Law governs land ownership, promotes mediation and reconciliation in resolving land disputes.[79] It provides a legal basis for mediation efforts and promotes consistency in outcomes.[80] Rwanda also integrates traditional Gacaca courts with modern legal structures that acknowledge and incorporate indigenous methods of conflict resolution.[81] The challenges faced by Rwanda include balancing traditional practices with modern legal frameworks to ensure that both are respected and integrated effectively.[82] Ensuring consistency and fairness in decisions made by community mediators from different areas is another challenge.[83]

5.9.3.1 Similarities

All three countries employ a mix of formal legal frameworks and traditional community-based mediation methods.[84] They therefore recognise the importance of involving local customs into dispute resolution.[85] Limited access to legal representation for disadvantaged communities is a shared challenge that has impact on fairness and inclusivity of mediation process.[86]

5.9.3.2 Differences

Rwanda's emphasis on community-driven Abunzi mediation is a highlighting feature that ensures localised and culturally sensitive dispute resolution.[87] South Africa's focus on addressing historical injustices such as land restitution makes it different as it emphasises the need for transformative and designed solutions.[88]

---

[78] Mutisi (2011), pp. 1–5.
[79] Rwanda's 2013 Land Law.
[80] Rwanda's 2013 Land Law.
[81] Rose (2003), p. 197.
[82] Chirayath et al. (2005), pp. 1–26.
[83] Polavarapu (2011), p. 105.
[84] Shewell (2020), pp. 1–3.
[85] Kariuki (2007), pp. 75–91.
[86] Djurfeldt (2020), p. 104305.
[87] Abbott (2014), pp. 1–10.
[88] Evans (2016), pp. 1–20.

5.10 Roles and Qualifications for Mediators in Each Country

Mediators play different roles in all three countries which are a reflection of the diverse approaches to mediation in different cultural, legal and social context. It is therefore necessary that we look at the roles played by mediators in each country and the qualifications they possess.

In South Africa mediators play an important role in court-annexed mediation by guiding parties through the mediation process in a formal legal system.[89] They also engage with community addressing land disputes combining formal and traditional approaches.[90] Mediators bridge the communication gap and ensure informed decisions are made.[91] Qualifications for mediators in South Africa often include a legal background for example qualified lawyers or retired judges.[92] Possession of legal knowledge is important in order to understand land laws and drafting legal agreements.[93] Mediators undergo accredited training involving mediation techniques, legal aspects of disputes and cultural sensitivity training.[94] Upon successful completion of training programs and examinations, mediator receives certification by recognized mediation bodies that ensure they meet professional standards.[95]

Mediators in Kenya work to identify common ground between parties.[96] Their role is to encourage disputing parties to reach mutually acceptable agreement by emphasising cooperation and compromise.[97] They also undergo training programs which lead to certification upon completion.[98] Kenyan mediators possess legal knowledge to navigate legal complexities related to land dispute.[99]

Mediators in Rwanda promote reconciliation and are expected to be culturally sensitive by understanding local customs and traditions.[100] Mediators receive training from local authorities and government bodies that focus on conflict resolution techniques.[101] Recognition by the community is also important. The Rwandan

89 Olivier (2018), pp. 1–100.

90 Olivier (2018), pp. 1–100.

91 Nolan-Haley (1998), p. 775.

92 Greyvenstein (2022), pp. 70–71.

93 Greyvenstein (2022), p. 70–71.

94 Blankey et al. (2024), p. 1.

95 Feasley (2011), p. 333.

96 Mugo (2017), p. 1.

97 Owiti (2009), pp. 1–16.

98 Keli (2018), p. 241.

99 Mugo (2017), p. 1.

100 Payne (2011).

101 Madukwe and Corps (2022).

government is responsible for supporting and overseeing the training and appointment of community mediators to ensure a standardised approach.[102]

5.11 Conclusion

In conclusion Rwanda's community-based approach shows effectiveness of involving local communities directly in mediation process, providing a sense of ownership and cultural relevance.[103] Kenya's integration of traditional and formal methods provides a comprehensive approach that ensures flexibility and adaptability for all contexts.[104] South Africa's focus on transformation gives a valuable lesson in addressing deep rooted historical injustices emphasising restitution and acknowledging mediation of land disputes.[105] Effective communication between formal and traditional systems is in this context important. While there are common challenges, each nation's unique emphasis on community involvement, a hybrid of traditional and formal methods or historical justice provides valuable insights for shaping land dispute resolution strategies on a global scale. While legal expertise is important, cultural sensitivity of mediators and government support for a standardized training play a huge role in ensuring effective mediation processes.

References

Abbott P (2014) The constant quest for solutions through dialogue and consensus in Rwanda: the mechanisms for dialogue and consensus. Institute of Policy Analysis and Research-Rwanda, Kigali

Al-Amin M, Akter R (2022) Land and conflict in Balovpur village: the role of land mediation

Alden Wily L (2018) The community land act in Kenya opportunities and challenges for communities. Land 7(1):12

Allen M (2014) Land and conflict in Papua New Guinea; the role of land mediation. Secur Challenges 10(2):1–14

Andrew JS (2003) Potential application of mediation to land use conflicts in small-scale mining. J Clean Prod 11(2):117–130

Antes JR et al (1998) Is stage model of mediation necessary. Mediation Q 16:287

Basita G (2001) Cross-cultural approach to resolving conflicts: Traditional mediation in Burundi compared to Western techniques. PhD dissertation, University of Duquesne

Betts W (1999) Third party mediation: an obstacle to peace in Nagorno Karabakh. SAIS Rev:161–183

Blankey K et al (2024) Alternative dispute resolution in agency administrative programs. J Disp Resol:1

[102] Payne (2011).

[103] Doughty (2014), pp. 780–794.

[104] Mtuku et al. (2022), pp. 1–19.

[105] Gross (2004), p. 47.

Blench R et al (2006) The role of traditional rulers in conflict prevention and mediation in Nigeria (Study prepared for the United kingdom's Department for international Development, Nigeria
Bob U (2010) Land –related conflicts in sub-Saharan Africa. Afr J Conflict Resolution 10(2)
Boulle L, Rycroft A (1998) Mediation: principles, process, practice. J South Afr Law:167
Bourdier F (2019) From confrontation to mediation: Cambodian farmers expelled by a Vietnamese company. J Curr Southeast Asian Aff 38(1):55–76
Caser U et al (2017) Environmental mediation: an instrument for collaborative decision making in territorial planning. Finisterra 52(104):109120
Chirayath L et al (2005) Customary law and policy reform: engaging with the plurality of justice systems
Cousins B, Kepe T (2004) Decentralisation when land and resource rights are deeply contested: a case study of the Mkambati eco-tourism project on the wild coast of South Africa. Eur J Coast South Africa 16(1):41–54
Derevyanko B et al (2023) Legal foundations for resolving land disputes through mediation as an alternative dispute resolution method. Eur Energy Environ Law Rev 32(5):248–256
Dhiaulhaq A et al (2015) The use and effectiveness of mediation in forest and land conflict transformation in Southeast Asia: case studies from Cambodia, Indonesia and Thailand. Environ Sci Pol 45:132–145
Dhiaulhaq A et al (2018) Resolving industrial plantation conflicts in Indonesia: can mediation deliver? Forest Policy Econ 91:64–72
Di X (2009) The developing trend of the people's mediation in China. Sociol Focus 42(3):288–245
Djurfeldt AA (2020) Gendered land rights, legal reform and social norms in the context of land fragmentation-a review of the literature for Kenya, Rwanda and Uganda. Land Use Policy 90: 104305
Doughty KC (2014) Our goal is not to punish but to reconcile: mediation in post-genocide Rwanda. Am Anthropol 116(4):780–794
Elliot MLP (1999) The role of facilitators, mediators, and other consensus-building practitioners. The consensus building handbook: A comprehensive guide to reaching agreement pp. 199–240
Engel A, Korf B (2005) Negotiation and mediation techniques for natural resource management. Food and Agriculture Organization of the United Nations, Rome, p 3
Evans M (2016) Structural violence, socioeconomic rights, and transformative justice. J Human Rights 15(1):1–20
Feasley A (2011) Regulating mediator qualifications in the 2008 EU mediation directive: the need for a supranational standard. J Disp Resol:333
Final Report of the Presidential Advisory Panel on Land Reform and Agriculture 2019
Geldenhuys K (2017) Specialised courts: a court for almost every occasion. Servamus Community-Based Safety Secur Magazine 110(3):20–24
Gibson JL (2009) Overcoming historical injustices; land reconciliation in South Africa. Cambridge University Press, Cambridge
Girke NC (2015) A matter of balance: the European Union as a mediator in Yemen. Eur Secur 24(4):509–524
Gren NM (2016) The principles of mediation. J E Eur Law:75
Greyvenstein L (2022) Mediation & the law: accreditation and training of family mediators. Servamus Community-Based Safety Secur Magazine 115(8):70–71
Gross AM (2004) The constitution, reconciliation, and transitional justice: lessons from South Africa and Israel. Stand J Int Law 40:47
Hansen T (2003) The narrative approach to mediation. Pepp Disp Resol Law J 4:297
Hertig YL (2004) Cross –cultural mediation: from exclusion to inclusion. Mission in acts: ancient narrative in contemporary context 59–72
Issaka SA (2023) Gender disparities in land rights a myth or a reality? Case studies of the situations in Kenya and Tanzania. J Econ Analysis 2(3):141–152
Jones TS (2001) Mediating with heart in mind: addressing emotion in mediation practice. Negot J 17(3):217–244

Kariuki F (2007) African traditional justice systems. Asia Pac J Anthropol 8:75–91

Keli J (2018) Mediation as a profession Kenya: A call for regulation. Alternative Dispute Resolution p. 241

Land Registration Act of 2012, South Africa

Lempereur A et al (2021) Mediation: negotiation by other moves. John Wiley & Sons, New York

MacDonnell LJ (1988) Natural resources dispute resolution: an overview. Nat Resour J 28(5)

Madukwe M, Corps M (2022) Can mediation reduce violence?

Mckersie RB et al (2004) Kaiser Permanente: using interest-based negotiations to craft a new collective bargaining agreement. Negot J 20(1):13–35

Mtuku B et al (2022) Formal justice and alternative dispute resolution on land based conflicts in Kenya. Int J Gender Stud 7(1):1–19

Mugo AK (2017) The applicability of mediation in the resolution of criminal disputes in Kenya: a case for restorative justice in the criminal justice system. Strathmore University, Nairobi

Muigai K (2017) Institutionalising traditional dispute resolution mechanisms and other community justice systems. Research Methods Africa Center for Technology Studies

Mutisi M (2011) The abunzi mediation in Rwanda: Opportunities for engaging with traditional institutions of conflict resolution.1–5

Mwaura RM (2016) An analysis of the viability of implementing the proposed small claims courts in the Kenyan judiciary

Narain V (2019) Bonds, battles and social capital: power and the mediation of water insecurity in peri-urban Gurgaon. India Water 11(8):1607

Nolan-Haley JM (1998) Informed consent in mediation: a guiding principle for truly educated decision making. Notre Dame Law Rev 74:775

Ntsebeza L (2007) The land question in South Africa: the challenge of transformation and redistribution. HSRC press, Schotschekloof

Nussbaum L (2016) Mediation as regulation: expanding state governance over private disputes. Utah Law Rev:361

Octaleny E et al (2020) Mediation of land disputes in South Sumatera Province. Annual Conference of Indonesian Association for Public Administration 21–39

Oleksik G et al (2014) Touch and gesture; mediating content display, inscriptions, and gestures across multiple devices. Pers Ubiquit Comput 18:1243–1257

Olivier M (2018) The role of court-annexed mediation in providing access to justice in the resolution of commercial disputes. PhD dissertation, University of North West

Owiti JDO (2009) An appraisal of mediation as an alternate dispute resolution in Kenya. Kampala International University, College of Humanities and Social Sciences, Kampala

Payne G (2011) Land issues in the Rwanda's post conflict law reform. Local Case Stud Afr Land Law:21–28

Polavarapu A (2011) Procuring meaningful land rights for the women of Rwanda. Yale Human Rights Dev Law J 14:105

Puri S et al (2004) Contextuality of participation in IS design: a developing country perspective. In Proceedings of the eighth conference on Participatory design: Artful integration: interweaving media, materials and practices, 2004

Rose LL (2003) Women's land access in post-conflict Rwanda: bridging the gap between customary land law and pending land legislation. Tex J Women Law 13:197

Rwanda's 2013 Land Law

Shamir Y (2016) Alternative dispute resolution approaches and their application

Shewell EA (2020) Mediation as a tool for conflict transformation: A comparative analysis of the South African Truth and Reconciliation Commission and the Rwandan Gacaca courts. PhD dissertation, Stellenbosch University

The Constitution of the Republic of South Africa (1996)

The Land Act of 2012, South Africa

The Land Reform Act of 1996

van Hemert KM (2019) Justice on the grass: Reconciliation or exclusion? A study of Rwandan nation-building through local justice. BS thesis
Viscidi L, Fargo J (2015) Local conflicts and natural resources. A balancing act for Latin American governmants. Inter-American Dialogue
Wambua PM (2013) The challenges of implementing ADR as an alternative mode of access to justice in Kenya. Alternative Dispute Resolution 15
Wehrmann B (2008) Land conflicts: a practical guide to dealing with land disputes. Eschborn, GTZl
Yanto YD (2023) The effectiveness of mediation in resolving land disputes at the National Land Agency of Banyumas District. Proc Series Soc Sci Human 14:370–376
Zhang M et al (2024) Spatio-temporal characteristics and influencing factors of land disputes in China: do socio-economic factors matter? Ecol Indic 160:111938
Zhomartkyzy M (2023) Mediation and indigenous conflict resolution practices: Lessons from global indigenous communities. p. 230

Mmakgoedi Sylvia Rakgwale born in 1996. She is am currently employed at Road Accident Fund as an administrative assistant, passionate about the academic aspect of the legal field and helping people. She obtained her LLB at the University of Limpopo and did her practical legal training at Polokwane Law School where she shortly after wrote and passed her entire Attorney's Board Exams. She also studied a postgraduate short course in Anti-corruption and Commercial Crime Investigation with the University of South Africa (Unisa).She completed her LLM in Alternative Dispute Resolution with the University of Pretoria.

Chapter 6
A Review of the Role of Legal Counseling in Effective Mediation

Linda Ndebele

6.1 Introduction

This chapter provides a comprehensive examination of mediation, detailing its practical implementation within the South African justice system. Also, to be addressed are legislative and procedural guidelines applicable to mediation in South Africa. Through an examination of case law, this chapter examines the way legal counseling facilitates access to justice through mediation.

6.2 General Overview of Mediation in South Africa

Mediation, just like all other forms of alternative dispute resolution processes is aimed at improving the efficiency of dispute resolution by *inter alia* promoting constructive engagement between the parties and relieving mainstream courts of huge workloads created by litigious cases.[1] One of the key weaknesses of the mainstream adversarial justice system, largely applied by the South African courts, is that it creates opportunity for abuse by some litigants and legal counsel which ultimately frustrates the weaker party's effective access to justice.[2]

This chapter is based on the academic debate constructed in the LLM research dissertation by the author, L Ndebele on the UP Law repository website.

[1]Lavi (2018), p. 4.
[2]Lavi (2018), p. 4.

L. Ndebele (✉)
University of Pretoria, Pretoria, South Africa
e-mail: linda@ndpatt.co.za

R. Baboolal Frank (ed.), *Dispute Resolution within Africa*,
https://doi.org/10.1007/978-3-031-76261-1_6

Factors such as financial discrepancies between parties can easily be exploited to the extent that it can frustrate the weaker party's access to justice.[3] Access to justice must be sacrosanct for any justice system to function effectively.[4] Legal processes followed by the courts and other tribunals must be structured in a manner which promotes key outcomes such as fairness, efficiency, cost effectiveness and judicial independence.[5]

A society achieves effective access to justice when laws and legal procedure are not only codified but are also consistently applied for purposes of efficiently resolving legal disputes.[6] The South African Constitution,[7] is one of the key instruments used by our justice system to guarantee the right to access to justice.[8] It is structured to safeguard restorative justice and ensure that social unity is achieved by ensuring that legal disputes are resolved efficiently by applying the law effectively.[9] The Constitution also seeks to ensure that courts and other tribunals are empowered to hear and decide disputes effectively and in a manner that promotes access to justice by all.[10]

Access to the abovementioned courts and tribunals specified in the Constitution, however, is to a larger extent dependent on the parties' ability to afford legal counseling services especially in the higher court litigation process.[11] This arises from the fact that, despite the Constitution's objective of facilitating universal access to the judiciary, the provision of pro bono legal assistance in South Africa, particularly in civil cases, is not guaranteed.[12]

As much as the Constitution provides for parties to represent themselves, most times the intricacies of the law and strict court procedures makes it difficult for parties to effectively access the courts and justice as a whole without legal counsel who come at a cost.[13] The adversarial set up of the court process is mostly challenging for an unrepresented person.[14] As such, most people are largely reliant on legal counsel to assist them to properly access justice and enforce their rights against others.

There are however some organisations such as the Legal Aid South Africa established in terms of the Legal Aid South Africa Act,[15] which facilitate access to

---

[3] Lavi (2018), p. 4.

[4] Winlock (2005), p. 43.

[5] Winlock (2005), p. 43.

[6] Winlock (2005), p. 43.

[7] Act 108 of 1996.

[8] Act 108 of 1996.

[9] Act 108 of 1996.

[10] Act 108 of 1996.

[11] McQuoid-Mason (1999), p. 234.

[12] McQuoid-Mason (1999), p. 234.

[13] Act 108 of 1996, section 38.

[14] McQuoid-Mason (1999), p. 244.

[15] Act 39 of 2014, section 3.

civil courts by *inter alia* providing legal education and information concerning legal rights and obligations to prepare a client to represent themselves.[16] However these organisations can only help a few minorities who qualify in terms of the set means test.[17] In a bid to further promote access to effective and efficient resolution of legal disputes in South Africa, there are other key legislative measures in place to complement the objectives of the South African Constitution.

The South African Law Reform Commission Act, as amended,[18] makes provision for the establishment of the South African Law Reform Commission (the Law Reform Commission).[19] This Law Reform Commission was established with the sole objective of preserving the rule of law in South Africa by, *inter alia,* organising and facilitating progressive transformation of the laws of South Africa.[20]

Of significant relevance to this study is the work which has been done to date by the Law Reform Commission in researching and advancing recommendations aimed at improving legal counseling and dispute resolution in the courts through alternative dispute resolution processes such as mediation.[21] From as early as July 1996, the Law Reform Commission has been investigating and driving the formal adoption of alternative dispute resolution processes in South Africa for purposes of addressing the challenge of adversarial, abrasive, long drawn litigation and overburdened courts.[22]

In terms of this research it was established that alternative dispute resolution processes actually present parties with an opportunity to resolve their legal issues through processes which are most suitable under the parties circumstances .[23] One of the key concerns raised with respect to the adversarial litigation system in South Africa is that most litigants find the process frustrating because the parties lose control of the process as they are mostly represented by legal counsel who speaks to the judges on the parties' behalf in complex legal jargon.[24]

In most instances, the parties also lose control of the process because they participate only in an indirect manner where they are limited to giving evidence only where applicable.[25] The trial process was also identified to limit the parties to discussing only key legal points and does not afford the parties an opportunity to ventilate broader issues which are deemed not legal.[26] Litigation was also deemed to be expensive in that the more the case is delayed or long drawn due to factors such as

[16] Act 39 of 2014, section 3.

[17] McQuoid-Mason (1999), p. 251.

[18] Act 19 of 1973.

[19] Act 19 of 1973, section 4.

[20] Act 19 of 1973 section 4.

[21] SA Law Reform Commission Project (2022), p. xiv.

[22] SA Law Commission Project 94 (1997).

[23] SA Law Commission Project 94 (1997), p. 13.

[24] SA Law Commission Project 94 (1997), p. 13.

[25] SA Law Commission Project 94 (1997), p. 13.

[26] SA Law Commission Project 94 (1997), p. 13.

the complexity of the case, the more costly it is for the parties, which effectively affects the parties' financial access to justice.[27]

The society is changing at an extremely fast pace and thus it is trite that the South African Justice system and legal counseling approaches ought to develop and implement alternative dispute resolution mechanisms to match these changes thereof.[28] Mediation is identified by the Law Reform Commission as one of the substantial dispute resolution alternatives, which, if properly formalised and implemented has the potential to offer a notably efficient and less expensive avenue of resolving a dispute than adversarial litigation.[29]

There is therefore a need in South Africa today, to facilitate increased use of mediation in legal counseling for purposes of improving access to justice for all by mitigating the abuse of process typical of the adversarial litigation system. Mediation is a notable means to improving access to justice as anticipated by the South African Constitution. It is a confidential process whereby the parties engage the assistance of a neutral third party to facilitate resolution of the dispute through constructive dialogue.[30] The duly appointed mediator assists the parties to simplify the dispute by identifying the relevant issues and to consider solutions mutually beneficial to the parties.[31]

Mediation is generally voluntary and is wholly dependent on the parties' commitment to discuss the issues in good faith.[32] It is therefore important to ensure that parties, through the legal counseling process, are properly educated about their rights as well as the availability of mediation as a viable dispute resolution process.[33] Confidentiality in the mediation process is compulsory and the parties are bound to this confidentiality in terms of a signed mediation agreement. In addition to the confidentiality requirement, the parties can agree to any other terms suitable for the facilitation of successful resolution of the dispute.[34]

This ensures that the parties can retain control of the process and own the outcome thereof. The discussions between the parties are without prejudice and as such information is exchanged solely for the purposes of attempting to present the other party with enough information to engage in the discussion in an informed manner and not meant to be used as evidence against the other party as is the case in the adversarial system.[35] This encourages the parties to consider each other's submissions for purposes of settling and not fighting or proving the other party wrong.[36]

[27] SA Law Commission Project 94(1997), p. 13.

[28] SA Law Commission Project 94 (1997), p. 20.

[29] SA Law Commission Project 94 (1997), p. 22.

[30] Lavi (2018), p. 4.

[31] Mantle (2017), p. 22.

[32] Mantle (2017), p. 22.

[33] Mantle (2017), p. 15.

[34] Menkel-Meadow (2020), p. 65.

[35] Menkel-Meadow (2020), p. 66.

[36] Menkel-Meadow (2020), p. 70.

The main essence of mediation is also to mitigate continued loss to the parties by facilitating speedy resolution and exploring mutually beneficial solutions to the dispute. The costs of mediation are usually split equally between the parties which in most instances is deemed to be fair.[37] The resolution in mediation results in a settlement agreement on the parties' own terms unlike the case where an order is imposed by a judge following litigation.

The success of mediation is premised on the parties' willingness to compromise and not win at the full expense of the other party.[38] One notable feature of mediation is that the mediator does not have to be a lawyer and can be anyone agreed upon by the parties.[39] This is largely beneficial where the dispute is of a technical nature. In that instance, the parties can agree to employ the services of someone who specializes in the subject area to assist the parties to negotiate a solution.[40] In most instances, this becomes cheaper in that the parties are presented with cheaper alternatives to legal fees as well as other expenses such as expert fees and extensive expert reports.

For example, parties to a divorce case can opt to make use of the services of a religious leader from their own religious organisation to mediate the dispute at no cost to them. The settlement agreement from this process can then be presented to legal counsel to formalise and submit to court to be confirmed as a court order.[41] Mediation not only promotes resolution of the dispute but goes further to allow the parties to deal with the underlying causes of the conflict as well. Unlike the adversarial litigation process, the parties can fully ventilate both the non-legal and legal issues between them for purposes of obtaining a holistic settlement agreement.[42]

The mediation procedure is deemed to present a platform where the parties willingly participate in the process based on common principles and for the purposes of settling the dispute without competition.[43] Mediation seeks to move away from a loser and winner position to a compromised outcome.[44] In essence the parties are encouraged to properly assess the benefits of resolving the dispute sooner other than employing more resources to fan long drawn litigation at the risk of losing the case completely.[45]

One of the advantages of the mediation process is that the parties are assisted by the mediator to identify and focus on their mutual interests which often encourages cooperation where each party sees an opportunity for their interests and rights to be

[37] Menkel-Meadow (2020), p. 80

[38] Mantle (2017), p. 25.

[39] Mantle (2017), p. 25.

[40] De Jong (2007), p. 286.

[41] Egan v Motor Services (Bath) Ltd (2007), para 52.

[42] *Egan* (2007), para 52.

[43] Fisher and Ury (2011), p. 16.

[44] Fisher and Ury (2011), p. 16.

[45] *MB v NB* (2010) (3) SA 220 para 55.

safeguarded.[46] The adversarial litigation process in most instances focuses more on proving correctness other than a compromise which encourages competition as both parties hope to win by convincing the judge that they are right, and the other party is wrong.[47]

The autonomy of mediation is also evident from the voluntary nature of the process.[48] The parties are not bound by strict procedural requirements and the need to make complex substantive arguments which renders the process simpler for unrepresented parties to understand.[49] The settlement agreement can be specific to the parties' standards and not to external non-negotiable norms imposed by courts in a court order.[50] The parties therefore have the opportunity to choose what is fair for them with the assistance and guidance of the mediator.

One of the significant roles of the litigation process is to expose the truth from the evidence presented by the parties. This is one of the key contributing factors to the lengthy procedure in trials because legal counsel must exhaustively present evidence to prove the case to the judge.[51] In mediation, the parties do not have to prove their cases but seek to understand each other for purposes of reaching a mutual compromise. This simplistic approach of mediation, however, may lead to the frustration of the party who sees his truth as not being properly ventilated. This inevitably results in that party walking away from the mediation process and resorting to further litigation thereafter which then lengthens the dispute resolution process.[52]

A case in point is the case of *Kalagadi Manganese (Pty) Ltd (Kalagadi) and others v Industrial Development Corporation (IDC) and others*.[53] In this case the IDC suggested that the parties engage in mediation in a bid to seek a financially sound solution to the issues in dispute. The parties then proceeded to conclude a written mediation agreement in terms of High Court Rule 41A of the Uniform Courts Rules.[54] However, before the mediation process could be concluded, the IDC withdrew from the process seemingly on the basis that it did not perceive that continuing with the process would yield meaningful outcomes for them.[55]

This led Kalagadi Manganese to accuse IDC of not mediating in good faith and prompted Kalagadi to bring an application to declare the withdrawal from mediation unlawful.[56] The Kgalagadi case thus defines and highlights importance of mediating in good faith. The court emphasised that the fact that the parties cannot agree or find

---

[46] Lavi (2018), p. 7.
[47] Lavi (2018), p. 7.
[48] Gren (2016), p. 75.
[49] Gren (2016), p. 78.
[50] Gren (2016), p. 79.
[51] Lavi 2018), p. 27.
[52] Lavi (2018), p. 27.
[53] (2021) ZAGPJHC 127.
[54] Kalagadi case (2021) para 5.
[55] Kalagadi case (2021) para 17.
[56] Kalagadi case (2021), para 8.

a resolution does not amount to mediating in bad faith.[57] This means the parties can freely engage in the mediation process without necessarily having to accept settlement options which are not beneficial to them. Parties are therefore free to withdraw from the mediation if there are no prospects that a suitable resolution will be achieved.[58]

The court in the Kalagadi case above was also required to decide on the publication and reliance on documents and information disclosed during the mediation process to prove a case in court. The court clearly emphasised the importance of confidentiality with respect to information and documentation exchanged by the parties in the mediation process. The Kalagadi case also highlights another key aspect with regards to appointing mediators in a strategic manner to create better chances of resolution in that process.[59]

Where the matter is complex, the parties can appoint more than one specialist mediator whom they trust enough to properly facilitate the dispute. In this case, the parties engaged former Chief Justice Moseneke and former judge, Advocate John Myburg to facilitate the mediation based on their vast commercial dispute resolution experience and knowledge.[60] The honorable judge Spilg in this case also highlighted another key advantage of mediation, which is that it suspends and stays all other proceedings to enable the parties to properly apply themselves to the negotiations.[61] However the success of the mediation process is thus totally dependent on the understanding and cooperation of the parties and their legal counselors and a willingness to trust each other enough to engage in *bona fide* discussions and compromise.[62]

The key to the success of mediation is intimately linked to the legal counseling process as will be discussed in this chapter.[63] The disadvantages of mediation are beyond the scope of this research. Legislative guidelines to mediation and to the legal counseling process are key to achieving effective resolution of disputes through mediation. The legislative framework of mediation in South Africa today is discussed herein below.

---

[57] Kalagadi case (2021), para 17.

[58] Kalagadi case (2021), para 30.

[59] Kalagadi case (2021), para 30.

[60] Kalagadi case (2021), para 7.

[61] Kalagadi case (2021), para 11.

[62] Marumoagae (2016), pp. 41–57.

[63] Mantle (2017), p. 76.

6.3 Legal Framework of Mediation in South Africa

Over the past few years, there have been significant strides to incorporate mediation in Legal Education and Development training courses in South Africa.[64] The academic fraternity has also been largely contributing to the advancement of the mediation process through the development of affordable and accessible training programs to supplement the legal counseling skills of key players in the justice system such as judges and legal counselors.[65] Higher education institutions such as the University of Pretoria now offer mediation training courses structured to educate legal counsel and other professionals in the field of mediation.

The abovementioned courses are meant to assist legal counselors as well as non-legal counselors in acquiring the necessary skills to assist them in effective mediation.[66] In addition to the above efforts there has also been the establishment of professional bodies such as the Dispute Settlement Accreditation Council (DSAC) which was created in South Africa during 2010.[67]

The sole objective of this organization is to outline and publish accreditation standards for dispute-resolution practitioners such as mediators in South Africa.[68] The DSAC also produces training material and offers training courses for alternative dispute resolution practitioners based on the standards set by the International Mediation Institute based in the Hague.[69] It is trite that the success of the mediation process is to a larger extent dependent on the professionalism and skills exhibited by the mediator. Organisations such as the Dispute Settlement Accreditation Council are available resources for mediators seeking proper training and accreditation on effective mediation practices suitable for the South African context. It also serves as a monitoring and oversight body for registered mediators.[70]

One of the initial attempts to incorporate and formalise mediation in the South African courts system was in terms of the *Short Process Courts and Mediation In Certain Civil Cases Act (The Mediation Act),*[71] which was intended to commence in 1992. This Act was promulgated for the purposes of *inter alia* providing for

[64] Legal Education and Development website, available at https://www.lssalead.org.za/course/civil-mediation-online-course/ accessed on 13 October 2023.

[65] Legal Education and Development website, available at https://www.lssalead.org.za/course/civil-mediation-online-course/ accessed on 13 October 2023.

[66] UP enterprises website available at https://www.enterprises.up.ac.za/mediation-training-course_afsa-11 accessed on 12 October 2023.

[67] DiSAC available at http://disac.co.za/wp-content/uploads/2014/12/DiSAC_-Code-of-Professional-Conduct-for-Mediators.pdf accessed on 1 November 2023.

[68] DiSAC available at http://disac.co.za/wp-content/uploads/2014/12/DiSAC_-Code-of-Professional-Conduct-for-Mediators.pdf accessed on 1 November 2023.

[69] https://imimediation.org/about/ accessed on 1 November 2023.

[70] DiSAC Code of Professional Conduct for Mediators accessed at http://disac.co.za/wp-content/uploads/2014/12/DiSAC_-Code-of-Professional-Conduct-for-Mediators.pdf 1.

[71] Act 103 of 1991.

mediation in certain civil cases in the Magistrates' Court and established a formalised mediation process for the lower courts.[72]

In terms of section 2 of this Act, qualified members of the Association of Law Societies of the Republic of South Africa, the General Bar Council of South Africa and the Department of Justice could be sworn in to the office of mediator by the senior Magistrate in their respective jurisdiction to act as mediators in that magisterial court jurisdiction.[73] The Mediation Act in section 3, allowed parties or their legal counsel to apply for a dispute to be referred to mediation at any stage prior to the issuing of summons. Further, this Act provided for the parties or their legal counsel to refer a dispute to mediation after summons has been issued but before judgment has been granted.[74]

In terms of this Act, section 3 (1)(a)(ii), the court was empowered to grant an adjournment to allow for mediation only if it is satisfied that such mediation attempts will not delay the finalisation of the matter or prejudice any of the parties.[75] Mediation under this Act was meant to be conducted at court and in chambers before the mediator.[76] This Act however was never implemented and remains un repealed.[77] More efforts continue to be made to formalise and incorporate mediation in the District and Regional Magistrates Courts in South Africa through the introduction of the Court Annexed mediation project in 2014.

In terms of section 71 of the Mediation rules,[78] regulating this court annexed mediation, the main objective of mediation is to promote access to justice and to promote restorative justice. Another key objective is to preserve relationships between the parties to the dispute.[79] Court annexed mediation is meant to provide litigants with a resolution option which extends beyond the legal scope of magistrates and to facilitate a speedy and cost-effective dispute resolution alternative.[80] As with the above Mediation Act, mediators were appointed to complement the functioning of magistrates in specific magisterial jurisdictions. Despite the appointment of these mediators and publication of the readiness of the court annexed mediation process by the department of Justice, same was suspended with effect from the 15th of March 2022 indefinitely.[81]

[72] Act 103 of 1991.

[73] Act 103 of 1991.

[74] Act 103 of 1991.

[75] Act 103 of 1991.

[76] Act 103 of 1991.

[77] Hutchison and Porter-Wright (2018), p. 338.

[78] Rules of Court: Amendment: Mediation Chapter 2, G 37448 RG 10151 GN 183, 18 Mar 2014.

[79] 2014 amendment of rules regulating the conduct of the proceedings of the Magistrates Court of South Africa.

[80] 2014 Amendment of Rules regulating the conduct of the proceedings of the Magistrates Court of South Africa.

[81] https://www.justice.gov.za/mediation/mediation.html accessed on 1 November 2023.

Similar to the aforementioned discussion on the Short Process Courts and Mediation In Certain Civil Cases Act, no justifications have been provided for the cessation of this significant court annexed mediation initiative that would have provided substantial benefits to the general populace in the overburdened Magistrate's courts. Some scholars have attributed these failures to implement mediation to a combination of factors such as lack of political will to provide the necessary funding to ensure that these legislative provisions are successfully implemented.[82]

Other scholars attribute it to a deemed resistance by legal counsel who simply ignore the mediation process and continue to pursue the adversarial litigation system which they are properly trained for.[83] There are also those scholars who believe that there is a general resistance to alternative dispute resolution processes in a bid to protect the development of the law through legal precedent.[84] A case in point dealing with the reluctance of legal counsel and parties to implement mediation before attempting litigation is the Constitutional court case of *Port Elizabeth Municipality v Various Occupiers.*[85] In this case, the parties failed to mediate the dispute as provided for in terms of section 7 of the Prevention of Illegal Eviction from and Unlawful Occupation of Land Act (PIE).[86]

The court was *inter alia* required to decide whether it is appropriate for the court to direct the parties to attend to mediation in an appeal court after they have failed to do so in the court of first instance. The court found that a failure to mediate at the earliest possible opportunity can prejudice the process because by the time a case gets to appeal, some advantages of mediation such as saving costs and preserving the relationship between the parties have already been defeated and thus mediation is unlikely to succeed.[87] However, the court also found that the failure to mediate, in the context of the PIE Act will determine whether the eviction itself is just and equitable.[88]

Section 7 of PIE provides for mediation and negotiation before a matter can be referred to litigation. In terms of section 7(1), where the municipality is not the owner of the land in dispute, the municipality is empowered to appoint experts in dispute resolution to *inter alia* attempt to mediate and settle the dispute before referring to litigation.[89] In terms of section 7(2), where the municipality is not the owner of the land in dispute, the member of the Executive Council designated by the Premier of the province concerned may appoint mediators to attempt to mediate and settle any dispute in terms of this Act.[90]

---

[82] Hutchinson and Porter-Wright (2018), p. 334.

[83] Hutchison and Porter-Wright (2018), p. 337.

[84] Hutchinson and Porter-Wright (2018), p. 334.

[85] 2005 (1) SA 217 (CC).

[86] Act 19 of 1998.

[87] *Port Elizabeth Municipality* (2005) para 47.

[88] *Port Elizabeth Municipality* (2005) para 47.

[89] Act 19 of 1998.

[90] Act 19 of 1998.

Despite the existence of these mediation provisions, legal counsel had not mediated the dispute before approaching the High Court. Judge Sachs remarked that our modern legal systems are transitioning to compel parties to participate in the mediation process.[91] This is beneficial to the parties even if settlements are not achieved in that mediation because it can avoid exacerbation of tensions which are characteristic of the litigation process in addition to saving costs.[92]

There are many other legislative provisions in South Africa which formalise mediation such as the Mediation of Certain Divorce Cases Act,[93] and the Commission for Conciliation and Mediation in South Africa established in terms of section 112 of the Labor Relations Act.[94] However, key to this study is the latest attempt to formalise mediation in the High Courts of South Africa through the amendment of the Uniform Rules of Court to incorporate a new rule 41A.[95] In terms of this rule 41 A (1), mediation is legally defined as a voluntary process whereby the litigants agree to appoint an unbiassed mediator to assist the parties to resolve the dispute between them.[96]

The mediator in terms of the abovementioned court rule may also assist the parties to identify issues in dispute and the issues which are no longer disputed and can be settled.[97] The role of the mediator is to assist the parties to craft a settlement agreement after they have jointly considered possible compromise options. In terms of this rule 41, the mediator can also assist the parties to simplify their priorities through amicable discussions with the hope to ultimately resolve the dispute.[98]

The legal definition of mediation in Rule 41 A above is very significant because it provides a broad meaning of the application of mediation in South Africa. Of note is the fact that the parties do not have to agree on all aspects of the case but can settle what they can and refer the balance of the issues to trial.[99] The parties are therefore required to earnestly assess their dispute for purposes of attempting to settle as much of the case as they can by *inter alia* exploring other options to resolve the issues in dispute until they reach a compromise.[100]

One practical way of properly applying rule 41 A (1) is to engage an expert like a doctor to be a mediator in a medical dispute as opposed to engaging him as a witness in a lengthy trial. The way this rule 41 (A) (1) is structured, encourages earnest engagement without necessarily forcing the parties to compromise to their

---

[91] *Port Elizabeth Municipality* (2005) para 40.

[92] *Port Elizabeth Municipality* (2005) para 42.

[93] Act 24 of 1987.

[94] Act 66 of 1995.

[95] Act 59 of 1959—Uniform Rules of Court amendment (19 June 2023).

[96] Act 59 of 1959.

[97] Act 59 of 1959.

[98] Act 59 of 1959.

[99] Act 59 of 1959.

[100] Act 59 of 1959.

detriment.[101] It is noteworthy that the mediation process and outcomes remain confidential and do not form part of the court record, and the mediation is conducted independent of the court itself. The parties are thus not compromised by complying with the requirement to mediate in terms of this rule.[102]

The application of Rule 41A is more fully illustrated in the case of *The Industrial Development Corporation ("the IDC") v Kalagadi Manganese (Pty) Ltd ("Kalagadi").*[103] In this case, the court found that the judicially sanctioned Rule 41 A imposes a legal duty on all the parties to diligently participate in the mediation process and that refusal to comply with this requirement without just cause can attract adverse costs and consequences for the party at fault.[104]

The above case also clarifies that an unwilling party cannot be compelled to mediate, and the parties are not forced to reach an agreement. The success of the mediation process itself is therefore entirely dependent on the party's commitment to a compromised solution.[105] The court also notes that the parties in terms of Rule 41 are protected from unnecessary delays in that the mediation process must be concluded within 30 days. In exceptional cases where the parties require more time to discuss, they may apply to the court for extension upon good cause shown. Similarly, where a party is not cooperating, the other party is not bound to wait until the expiry of the 30-day period to proceed with litigation.[106] The affected party can withdraw from the mediation and set the matter down for hearing prior to the expiry of the 30-day period.

6.4 The Role of Legal Counseling in the Mediation Process

Despite the significant developments in mediation discussed above, the issue of long drawn litigation remains a real problem in both the High and Lower Courts in South Africa. There is therefore a need to critically assess the legal counseling process in the context of mediation processes which have been established especially because of the growing concerns expressed by *inter alia* Judges, members of the legal fraternity as well as the public about the impact of legal counseling in mediation.[107]

As can be gleaned from case law discussed above, the voluntary nature of mediation creates room for the parties and legal counsel to ignore same even where it is the most effective way to resolve the dispute. This study presupposes

[101] Act 59 of 1959.

[102] Act 59 of 1959.

[103] *Kalagadi* (2021) para 28.

[104] *Kalagadi* (2021) para 28.

[105] *Kalagadi* (2021) para 30.

[106] *Kalagadi* (2021) para 30.

[107] *MB* (2010) para 48.

that the legal counselor is autonomous and that the clients act in accordance with the legal advice rendered (The lawyer autonomy model).[108]

In order to advise the client constructively, in terms of this model, the legal counsel must also consider moral, economic, social as well as political factors which are relevant to the client's facts.[109] On the whole, the legal counselor is obliged to also exhaustively assess and carefully consider other relevant factors which may facilitate effective dispute resolution and access to justice such as mediation.[110] In addition to legislative efforts as discussed in this study, it is imperative that legal counsel and judicial officers must be fully committed to the proper implementation of mediation in our justice system process.[111]

In terms of section 3.10 of the South African Legal Council Code of Conduct,[112] legal counsel is obliged to adopt effective dispute resolution options. They are mandated to advise their clients, at the earliest possible opportunity about the likely success of the clients' case and not to persist with a case which has no merits.[113] It is unethical and unprofessional for legal counsel to generate unnecessary work for themselves and in so doing raise unnecessary legal expenses for their clients.[114] Failing to properly advise a client of the option to mediate is potentially a violation of this rule and it is trite that legal counsel must be held accountable in this regard to ensure that they do not become an unnecessary hinderance to mediation at the expense of the client.[115]

Judicial response to Legal counsel's reluctance or refusal to engage in mediation by granting adverse cost orders is a key driver to the adoption of mediation by legal counsel.[116] In the case of *MB v NB (Brownlee v Brownlee)*,[117] the court reiterates that legal counsel at times fall short of the duty to act professionally as officers of the court who must always display objectivity and well calculated value judgement.[118] It is this well calculated value judgement which is key to effective mediation. Instead of using the law to facilitate constructive dispute resolution processes such as mediation, legal counsel sometimes employs the law as a weapon to ensure that the winner takes all. This approach inevitably frustrates the adoption of the mediation process and the benefits which the parties could obtain from same.[119]

---

[108] Green (1998), p. 1801.
[109] Green (1998), p. 1801.
[110] Hausman (1990), pp. 383–402.
[111] Hausman (1990), p. 384.
[112] Act 28 of 2014 sec 36(1).
[113] Act 28 of 2014 sec 36(1).
[114] Act 28 of 2014.
[115] Hutchison and Porter-Wright (2018), p. 338.
[116] Hutchison and Porter-Wright (2018), p. 338.
[117] *MB* (2010) para 53.
[118] *MB* (2010) para 48.
[119] *MB* (2010) para 53.

In the *MB v NB* case, judge Brassey criticised the manner in which this cc Five Hundred Thousand Rands.[120] Although the legal counsel is said to have followed court process and managed the case well for adversarial litigation purposes, the judge was of the view that this case was more suited for referral to mediation and that legal counsel ought to have adopted that mediatory approach.[121]

The judge noted with concern that the school fees and the maintenance which the parties were fighting about could have been significantly reduced by the Five Hundred Thousand Rands which was ultimately paid by the parties in respect of legal fees.[122] Agreeing to allocate this money to maintenance at the commencement of the case through mediation would have been more beneficial to the minor child and would have mitigated the resultant damage to the parties' relationship through the long-drawn abrasive adversarial approach.

In a country where there is a real issue of overcrowding of the courts, it is imperative that parties and legal counsel must commit more to engaging in mediation so that the courts may apply resources to more complex matters which do not qualify for mediation such as public interests' disputes.[123] Section 34 of the Constitution guarantees everyone's right to have any dispute that can be resolved by the application of law decided in a fair public hearing before a court or, where appropriate, another independent and impartial tribunal or forum.[124] It is therefore imperative for legal counsel to ensure that suitable cases are referred to appropriate mediation forums where they can potentially be finalised speedily in order to protect the clients' rights in terms of section 34 of the Constitution. In a bid to also give effect to the provisions of section 34, the courts have structures to oversee the overall management of cases by legal counsel and all relevant parties through the case management system.[125]

Judges are increasingly rebuking and calling out the conduct of legal counsel who frustrate effective and efficient resolution of disputes in the courts by imposing punitive costs orders with the hope to discourage such abusive conduct.[126] Legal counselors are officers of the court and are thus duty bound to conduct the legal counseling process in a manner that ensures the realisation of the rights enshrined in section 34 of the Constitution.[127]

Upon admission in the High Court as a legal counselor in South Africa, every legal counselor undertakes to facilitate access to justice and the interests of their clients above selfish interests. Selfish interests which are detrimental to

---

[120] *MB* (2010) para 48.

[121] *MB* (2010) para 48.

[122] V N D v V N J J (2023) *ZAGPPHC 612.*

[123] V N D (2023) para 612.

[124] Act 108 of 1996.

[125] Act 59 of 1959.

[126] *Tyibilika v MEC for Health, Eastern Cape Province* (2021) ZAECBHC 38.

[127] Act 28 of 2014.

administration of justice include but are not limited to a failure to manage personal emotions while conducting the legal counseling process, engaging in cases that the legal counselor is not fully knowledgeable about as well as financial greed.[128] These selfish interests also have the effect of frustrating the mediation process. It is imperative that legal counsel must at all material times ensure that they facilitate the fair resolution of disputes by ensuring effective and efficient client management. This entails proper explanation of the law to the client as well as managing client expectations by explaining the costs versus the benefits of pursuing a particular cause of action and resolution process.[129]

As a general rule, the initial step to legal counseling is to screen the purported instructions and to ensure that the legal counselor is properly skilled in that area of law and has the requisite experience required to competently assist the client and the court as a whole.[130] Legal counsel must properly consult with a client for purposes of understanding the facts and advising on best possible cause of action which is not only lawful but also benefits the client the most. The legal counsel must endeavor to establish a trust relationship with the client because this is the only way a client will cooperate in processes such as mediation.

When a client is content with the professional judgment of a legal counselor, they frequently adhere to the advice provided.[131] Legal counselors must always function as a representative of clients as well as custodians of the constitution with a specific duty to uphold and advance the highest quality of justice.[132] In addition to advising and defending the client's rights, legal counsel must also be effective negotiators and communicators.[133] The failure by the legal counselor to properly uphold these responsibilities all the time compromises the effectiveness of the mediation process and the administration of justice.

The judge in the Kalagadi case importantly noted that although mediation remains essentially voluntary in its nature, the courts are empowered to facilitate proper compliance with the requirement to mediate by issuing appropriate costs orders to discourage noncompliance.[134] The court made reference to the case of *Outar v Greno Industries,*[135] where the court found that the court cannot allow a litigant to choose to ignore established procedures of the court and legislation.[136] The court also cited the precedent set on the American case of *Del Fuoco v Wells*,[137]

---

[128] *V N D (2023) 612.*

[129] V N D (2023) 612.

[130] Dinovitzer et al. (2014), p. 667.

[131] Zacharias (2001), p. 214.

[132] Dinovitzer (2014), p. 667.

[133] Dinovitzer (2014), p. 667.

[134] *Kgalagadi* (2021) para 35.

[135] 2005 WL 238740(ND NY.Sep.27,2005) 3.

[136] *Kgalagadi* (2021) para 32.

[137] *Del Fuoco v. Wells,* 8:03-cv-161-T-23TGW (M.D. Fla. Jan. 4, 2007).

where the court granted an order against the plaintiff and his legal counsel for abusing the mediation process to extort settlement.[138]

The above challenges in the legal counseling process have led to the promulgation of rule 41 A (2) c, which formally regulates the requirement to consider mediation before commencing litigation in the normal course. While mediation remains generally voluntary in terms of this rule, there is a requirement for legal counsel to properly justify a refusal to mediate.[139] In this regard, Rule 41 A (2) c, clearly defines the specific notices to be issued, which notices must specify the reasons why a party believes that the dispute cannot be capable of being mediated.[140]

Further to the above, it is important to note that the court retain the right to compel legal counsel to refer the matter to mediation where it is in the interest of justice to do so.[141] In terms of Rule 41 (3) b, a Judge or a Case Management Judge may order the parties to consider referral of a dispute to mediation any time before judgement is granted. The abovementioned Rule 41(3) b, Rule 37 relating to the requirement to conduct pretrial conferences, as well as Rule 37A relating to judicial management complement each other to promote *bona fide* engagement between legal counsel to consider settlement before proceeding with a trial.[142]

One of the key points which legal counsel must discuss during a pretrial conference and judicial management is the possibility of settlement. To properly assess the possibility of settlement, the parties are required to properly engage in negotiation akin to mediation.[143] The pretrial process is intended to curtail the issues in the matter and ensure that the case is ready for trial, thereby eliminating delays.[144] In a bid to ensure that the legal counsel have conducted the pretrial conference in earnest, a case management judge is required to certify a case trial ready only in instances where the judge is satisfied that there exist triable issues and the case is ready for trial and that all issues that are amenable to being resolved without a trial have been dealt with.[145] The judge must also be satisfied that the remaining issues that are to go to trial have been adequately defined.[146]

[138] *Kalagadi* (2021) para 32.

[139] Act 59 of 1959.

[140] Act 59 of 1959.

[141] Act 59 of 1959.

[142] Act 59 of 1959.

[143] Act 59 of 1959.

[144] https://www.judiciary.org.za/images/news/2019/amendment_of_uniform_rules_of_court_with_the_insertion_of_case_management_rules page 1 accessed on 12 October 2023.

[145] *Tyibilika* (2021) para 38.

[146] *Tyibilika* (2021) para 38.

6.5 Discussion of the Practical Effects of Legal Counseling on Successful Implementation of Mediation to Minimise Unnecessary Litigation

Legal counseling plays a significant role in the effective use of mediation to curb the incidence of unnecessary, long drawn cases. This study has been largely influenced by some extreme cases where the attitudes of legal counsel to the mediation process have had detrimental effects to clients who have essentially lost valuable resources such as time and money. These cases have also cast doubt on the preparedness of most legal counsel to engage effectively in mediation in line with the recent legal developments.

In the case of *University of South Africa v Socikwa and Others*, the court notes in general that some the legal counsel's knowledge of the law and its application is lacking which is most embarrassing to the legal profession as a whole.[147] Proper knowledge of the facts and understanding of the law are key to effective dispute resolution. A case in point is the case of *Egan v Motor Services*[148] where Lady Justice Arden, expressed her displeasure at the legal counseling process exhibited by the legal counsel who argued this case. The learned judge was of the view that this dispute ought to have been effectively resolved through mediation.[149]

This case highlights main aspects of legal counseling such as proper management of client expectations, the need for legal counsel to do proper costs benefit analysis before pursuing a case as well as proper case management.[150] Most importantly, this case emphasises the need for legal counsel to make use of mediation in instances where it is the most beneficial resolution option to the client. In the context of this case, effective dispute resolution related to a cost-effective resolution of the case in a manner that is most beneficial to the parties so represented.[151]

This case of *Egan v Motor Services (Bath) Ltd*[152] is an unfortunate case where the parties' spent approximately One Hundred Thousand Pounds to resolve a case which was worth only 6000 Pounds.[153] This is a *locus classicus* case of ineffective dispute resolution apparently fueled by legal counsel and their disregard of available more constructive mediation. The litigants in this case essentially lost financially and their relationship was further broken down.

The legal counsel were the only winners in this instance as they obtained financial gain.[154] Where a client declines constructive legal advice, the legal counsel must

[147] (2023) 8 BLLR 836 (LC).

[148] *Egan v. Motor Services (Bath) Ltd, 2007 E.W.C.A. Civ 1002 (2007).* 52.

[149] *Egan* (2007) para 53.

[150] *Egan* (2007) para 53.

[151] *Egan* (2007) para 53.

[152] *Egan* (2007) para 53.

[153] *Egan* (2007) para 53.

[154] Stier (1991), p. *565*.

protect the sanctity of the profession by withdrawing from such a case.[155] A proper appreciation of the lawyer's role as a legal counselor must not be economic incentives which sometimes promote rather than discourage litigation. When legal counsel conducts themselves constructively, the effect is that the burden of case backlogs in the courts is mitigated. Further, access to justice becomes more effective and beneficial to society in that the economic and emotional burden which mostly is associated with litigation is reduced.[156]

Of note in the Egan case, was the judge's comments with regards to mediation being the best form of dispute resolution for this case. The judge was at pains to emphasise that effective legal counseling would have resulted in this case being referred for mediation.[157] There is therefore a clear nexus between effective mediation and the legal counseling approach adopted by the legal counselor. The judge importantly also stated that good quality legal counseling results in effective and efficient dispute resolution through mediation where it is clearly appropriate.[158]

The judge also emphasised that in this specific case, it would have been advisable for both the dealer and the client to seek the guidance of legal counsel to resolve the disagreement via negotiation rather than litigation. The judgment underscores the obligation of professional legal advisers to consistently maintain objectivity and provide accurate advice to clients, especially in situations when the client proves to be challenging.[159] The judge, in the comment above, reiterated the imperative duty of legal counsel to act rationally and promote beneficial legal representation. The learned judge correctly notes that it is not always easy for the legal counselor to persuade parties to mediate where they have strong feelings towards the case.[160] In instances where clients refuse to consider objective legal advice, it is the writer's view that counsel must withdraw than persist with abusive processes.

The relationship between the legal counselor and his or her client is pivotal to the effectiveness of mediation. Professional ethics are key to the manner in which the legal counselor executes his instructions. There is a non-negotiable duty for the legal counselor to adhere to the codes of professional conduct laid down by the profession throughout the legal counseling process.[161] There is a basic presumption that the legal counselor is knowledgeable of both substantive and procedural law and can advise client fully to such an extent that the client becomes fully informed and is able to furnish the legal counselor with informed instructions.[162] It is the responsibility of legal counsel to ensure that the client is adequately informed of the benefits and drawbacks of the dispute resolution process chosen, in addition to the costs thereof.[163]

---

155 Stier (1991), p. 566.
156 Edward (1982), p. 690.
157 *Egan* (2007).
158 *Egan* (2007).
159 *Egan* (2007).
160 *Egan* (2007).
161 Dinovitzer (2014), p. 663.
162 Zacharias (2001), p. 214.
163 Zacharias (2001), p. 218.

On the whole, effective legal counseling enhances access to justice by the society at large, because effective legal counseling mitigates the escalation of conflict between parties and encourages mutual cooperation.[164] Effective legal counselors are described as key lubricants which lessen the conflicts of our complex society.[165] This analogy is well suited because to most members of the public, their ability to fully access justice is with the assistance of legal counsel.

As can be gleaned from the *Egan* case discussed herein, sometimes legal counselors frustrate the intended outcomes of mediation due to a combination of factors such as financial benefit and a need to protect their own ego. Long drawn litigation provides more financial benefit to the legal counselor.[166] The judge in the *Egan* case above also clarified the role of the mediator and the opportunity afforded to the parties to seek a suitable mediator who has the skill to understand the technicality of the dispute. It is trite that the mediator must be skilled enough to properly assist the parties to define the issues in dispute and to facilitate the possibility of a compromised solution which will benefit both parties.[167] The judge also highlighted the massive saving of costs and time which the parties could have achieved by mediating the dispute. This is a crucial outcome of effective legal counseling and mediation which is most beneficial to the parties.[168] The judge in the Egan case also highlights that the best time to mediate is before the litigation begins.

Further, the learned judge also importantly notes that initiating negotiation or mediation in a case by legal counsel is not an indication of lack of knowledge or that the party has a weak case and is not confident of prospects of success. In fact, this is an ethical way to proceed where mediation is an appropriate option and therefore the judge encourages legal counsel to implement mediation more often to facilitate speedy dispute resolution.[169]

The above comment by the judge is particularly significant because the legal counselor is obligated to facilitate more constructive dispute resolution from the onset of a case by intentionally applying specific skills, attitudes and strategies which facilitate efficient resolution without compromising the rights of the client.[170] The judge above, implies that one of the reasons why legal counsel and parties may be reluctant to suggests and pursue mediation from the inception of a case is because they think that it is a sign of weakness.[171]

It is important for legal counsel to be trained and properly skilled so that they can shift from the traditional adversarial approach to cases. In the case of *MB v NB,*[172]

[164] Edward (1982), p. 690.

[165] Edward (1982), p. 691.

[166] Dinovitzer (2014), p. 663.

[167] *Egan* (2007) para 52.

[168] *Egan* (2007) para 52.

[169] *Egan* (2007) para 52.

[170] Redmount (1979), p. 181.

[171] *Egan* (2007) para 52.

[172] *MB* (2010) para 52.

Acting Judge Brassey emphasised that effective counseling entails a proper explanation to clients of available dispute resolution processes. The legal counselor must be properly skilled to apply the law to assist the client to do costs benefit analysis from the onset of a case.[173] Judge Brassey in this case indicated that he enquired from the Plaintiff whether she had been advised by her legal counsel about the availability of the mediation process and she indicated that she had not been advised.[174] The neglect by legal counsel to properly advise clients in this regard inevitably frustrates the opportunity for clients to resolve their disputes more amicably through mediation.

In the *MB v NB* case above, the learned judge highlights important advantages of mediation which include the fact that mediation can yield constructive outcomes especially when conducted by a well-trained mediator.[175] However, if clients are not advised in the legal counseling process, these advantages remain academic. This principle was also reiterated by judge Sachs in the case of *Port Elizabeth Municipality v Various Occupiers.*[176]

Legal counsel thus must be able to identify suitable experts who can advance successful mediation. This skill is obtained through training and knowledge of substantive law.[177] In this case of *MB v NB*, the learned judge also emphasised another important advantage of effective mediation, being that it is conducted under strict confidentiality. This is important because matters that are decided in courts can generally be published with the exception of sensitive cases such as cases relating to children.[178] It is the writer's opinion that if clients are properly conscientised about this advantage by their legal counselor, then in most cases they are encouraged to engage in mediation. This principle was also emphasised by the court in the *Kalagadi Manganese (Pty) Ltd and Others v Industrial Development Corporation of South Africa Ltd and Others case.*[179]

In the case of *Clemson v Clemson,*[180] the court emphasised the importance of due commitment by legal counsel to effective mediation. The court stated that there is an expectation on legal counsel to display objectivity and a high degree of common sense in the whole legal counseling process.[181] The court reiterated the expectation that legal counselors must not be so occupied in an adversarial approach to dispute resolution to the extent that they apply legal principles and court rules as weapons meant to fight and destroy their opponents.[182] This only fans long drawn litigation

[173] *MB* (2010) para 52.
[174] *MB* (2010) para 52.
[175] *MB* (2010) para 52.
[176] 2004 (12) BCLR 1268 (CC).
[177] *MB* (2010) para 50.
[178] *MB* (2010) para 52.
[179] [2021] ZAGPJHC 127 para 21.
[180] (2001) 1 All SA 622 W at 627 para 53.
[181] *Clemson* (2001) para 53.
[182] *Clemson* (2001) para 53.

and benefits only the legal counselors at the expense of the parties and ultimately frustrates the parties' right to have any dispute resolved in terms of section 34 of the Constitution.[183]

6.6 Conclusion

Overall, as can be gleaned from the caselaw discussed above, effective legal counseling as defined in this chapter is key to the realisation of the benefits of mediation to clients. Effective counseling is achieved when Legal counsel have proper substantive knowledge of the law and approach dispute resolution objectively. As can be gleaned from this Chapter, it is not sufficient to only enact legislation and structure legal processes which regulate the mediation process.

It is even more important to ensure that legal counsel, judges, and other officers of the court must work together to ensure that society benefits by accessing these dispute resolution alternatives timeously and effectively. The success of mediation, as can be gleaned from the *Kalagadi Manganese* case is solely dependent on the parties' and their legal counsel's commitment to attempting to mediate in good faith. Mediation in good faith entails attending to mediation diligently and ensuring that legal counsel and parties are properly prepared to engage in constructive discussion.

This however does not mean that parties are compelled to compromise to their detriment. Legal counsel needs to always remain ethical and put the needs of the client and access to justice above their own financial gain. While there are obvious indications in law, court rules, and legal precedent that efforts are being made to establish a formal legislative framework that promotes the use of mediation as an alternative to litigation in South Africa, further action is required to enhance the training of legal counsel. Further efforts are required to ensure that mediation platforms are effectively utilised to enhance access to justice, streamline conflict resolution procedures, and lessen the burden of lengthy court trials.

References

Books

Civil Mediation Online Course (2023). https://www.lssalead.org.za/course/civil-mediation-online-course/. Accessed 13 Oct 2023

Clemson v Clemson (2001) 1 All SA 622 W

De Jong M (2007) Divorce mediation in Australia: valuable lessons for family law reform in South Africa. Comp Int Law J Southern Africa 40(2):286

---

[183] *Clemson* (2001) para 53.

Del Fuoco v Wells, 8:03-cv-161-T-23TGW (M.D. Fla. Jan. 4, 2007)
Department of Justice and Constitutional Development (2023) Mediation. https://www.justice.gov.za/mediation/mediation.html. Accessed 1 Nov 2023
Dinovitzer R et al (2014) Reconsidering lawyer autonomy: the nexus between firm, lawyer, and client in large commercial practice. Am Bus Law J 51(3):667
Edward ED (1982) The lawyer as counselor and the prevention of litigation. Catholic Univ Law Rev 31(4):690
Egan v Motor Services (Bath) Ltd (2007)
Fisher R, Ury W (2011) Getting to yes: negotiating agreement without giving in, 3rd edn. Penguin Books, New York
Green BA et al (1998) Report of the working group on rendering legal assistance to similarly situated individuals. Fordham Law Rev 67:1801
Gren NM (2016) The principles of mediation. J Eastern Eur Law 24:75
Hausman A (1990) The ethics of lawyering in the public interest: using client and lawyer autonomy as a guidepost. Georgetown J Legal Ethics 4(2)
Hutchison A, Porter-Wright M (2018) Private ordering and dispute resolution. South Afr Law J 135(2):338
Judiciary of South Africa (2019) Amendment of uniform rules of court with the insertion of case management rules. https://www.judiciary.org.za/images/news/2019/amendment_of_uniform_rules_of_court_with_the_insertion_of_case_management_rules. Accessed 12 Oct 2023
Kalagadi Manganese (Pty) Ltd (Kalagadi) and others v Industrial Development Corporation (IDC) (2021) ZAGPJHC
Lavi D (2018) Alternative dispute resolution and domestic violence: women, divorce and alternative justice. Routledge, London
Mantle M (2017) Mediation: a practical guide for lawyers, 2nd edn. Edinburgh University Press Ltd., Edinburgh
Marumoagae C (2016) Does collaborative divorce have a place in south African divorce law? De Jure Law J 49(1):41–57
MB v NB (2010) (3) SA 220
McQuoid-Mason D (1999) Access to justice in South Africa. Windsor Yearb Access Justice 17:234
Menkel-Meadow C (2020) Mediation: practice, policy, and ethics. Aspen Publishing
Outar v Greno Industries 2005 WL 238740 (ND NY Sep. 27, 2005)
Port Elizabeth Municipality v Various Occupiers 2005 (1) SA 217 (CC)
Redmount RS (1979) An inquiry into legal counseling. J Leg Prof 4:181
SA Law Commission Project 94, Issue Paper 8 (1997) Alternative dispute resolution. https://www.justice.gov.za/salrc/ipapers/ip08_prj94_1997.pdf. Accessed 31 Oct 2023
SA Law Reform Commission Project 142 (2022) Investigation into legal fees -including access to justice and other interventions. https://www.saflii.org/za/other/ZALRC/2022/3.pdf. Accessed 31 Oct 2023
Stier S (1991) Legal ethics: the integrity thesis. Ohio State Law J 52(2):551
The 2014 amendment of rules regulating the conduct of the proceedings of the Magistrates Court of South Africa
The Constitution of the Republic of South Africa, 1996
The Legal Aid South Africa Act 39 of 2014
The Mediation of Certain Divorce Cases Act 24 of 1987
The Prevention of Illegal Eviction from and Unlawful Occupation of Land Act 19 of 1998
The Rules Board for Courts Law Act 107 of 1985, South Africa
The Rules of Court: Amendment: Mediation Chapter 2, G 37448 RG 10151 GoN 183, 18 March 2014
The Short Process Courts and Mediation in Certain Civil Cases Act 103 of 1991
The South African Dispute Settlement Accreditation Council (2011) Code of professional conduct for mediators. http://disac.co.za/wp-content/uploads/2014/12/DiSAC_-Code-of-Professional-Conduct-for-Mediators.pdf. Accessed 1 Nov 2023

The South African Law Reform Commission Act 19 of 1973
The South African Legal Council Code of Conduct Act 28 of 2014
Tyibilika v MEC for Health, Eastern Cape Province (2021) ZAECBHC
Uniform Rules of Court Act 59 of 1959, South Africa
University of South Africa v Socikwa and Others (2023) 8 BLLR 836 (LC)
V N D v V N J J (2023) ZAGPPHC 612
Winlock W (2005) The fundamental right of access to justice. East Afr Court Justice Human Rights Democracy 3:43
Zacharias F (2001) Limits on client autonomy in legal ethics regulation. Boston Univ Law Rev 81(1):214

Linda Tendesai Ndebele LLB—Rhodes University, LLM with distiction- University of Pretoria and currently enrolled for a Doctor of Laws degree at the University of Pretoria. She is a practising attorney in South Africa since 2012. She has a specific interest in legal counseling in family law practice. She is an accredited Family Law mediator since 2015 and is appointed as Court Annexed family law and civil law mediator in terms of rule 86 of the Court Annexed mediation rules in South Africa. She completed her research Masters in Alternative Dispute Resolution through the University of Pretoria.

Chapter 7
An Assessment of Africa As the Leader of Alternative Dispute Resolution

Chane Williamson

7.1 Introduction

This examines the function of reconciliation as a basis for mediation and conciliation in Africa in order to appraise Africa's role as a leader in dispute resolution. It will also examine Africa's regional and international arbitration institutions and will focus on Africa's future as a leader in dispute settlement.

Alternative dispute resolution and the art of reconciliation in Africa.

Many African individuals have lost trust in their countries' courts to resolve their concerns promptly or justly in a timely or just manner.[1] Because even "when courts are" approached, they may miss the underlying spark since they are not focused on conflict resolution or mitigation.[2] Galanter refers to judicial actions as having "radiating effects" that have an impact on society at large,[3] accentuating how disputes can sometimes be exacerbated by judicial decisions. Ernest Uwazie writes on a Nigerian lawyer's observation, "when the judge" declares "a winner, that is the beginning of the" actual struggle.[4] The ability of formal litigation, which is based on an adversarial process, to ensure fairness and satisfaction for disputants is limited.[5]

This inefficiency reflects the "in-between" condition of "African justice structures" in many circumstances.[6] Increasing litigation costs, which sometimes surpass

[1] Uwazie (2011), p. 1.

[2] Uwazie (2011), p. 2.

[3] Friedman (1989), p. 26.

[4] Uwazie (2011), p. 2.

[5] Alternative Dispute Resolution Practitioners Guide available at https://www.usaid.gov/sites/default/files/documents/1868/200sbe.pdf (accessed 8 June 2022).

[6] Uwazie (2011), p. 2.

C. Williamson (✉)
University of Pretoria, Pretoria, South Africa

R. Baboolal Frank (ed.), *Dispute Resolution within Africa*,
https://doi.org/10.1007/978-3-031-76261-1_7

the amount in dispute,[7] as well as failure to resolve disputes in a timely manner,[8] have fuelled the emergence of alternatives to the traditional litigation process.[9] It also costs disputants more in terms of time and money.[10] Contrary to formal court proceedings, alternative dispute resolution compromises a set of conflict-resolution techniques that are linked to operating outside of regular court litigation processes.[11] Unlike trials, which are formal procedures defined by rigorous regulations, mediation entails third party neutrals assisting conflicting parties in reaching an agreement.[12] When disputants believe their perspectives have been seriously addressed, they are more willing to settle and follow resolutions, since they respect the process's integrity and the opportunity to participate in it.[13]

The emphasis of mediation is generally on the parties' own interests rather than their negotiation positions.[14] It is intended to provide claimants with the opportunity "to have their" voices heard and to engage in "a process that satisfies all" parties in a way that a court case cannot.[15] Mediators who have been properly trained understand that the process is just as essential as the outcome.[16] Africa as a whole demonstrates the importance of the alternative dispute resolution process and its contribution to reconciliation.[17]

The concept of alternative dispute resolution is well-suited to traditional African justice notions, notably the essential value of reconciliation,[18] as well as the concept of Ubuntu. The goal isn't about 'winning', but rather the process of bringing contending parties together through reconciliation.[19] Reconciliation is at the heart of the African legal system, and restoring harmony is more vital than establishing the rule of law.[20] Much of what is done in post-conflict settings is based on the premise that healing is vital for reconciliation.[21] Various truth-and-reconciliation commissions, for example, were supposed to aid in the healing process.[22] it is assumed that

---

[7] Tahura (2018), p. 33.
[8] Uwazie (2011), p. 2.
[9] Tahura (2018), p. 33.
[10] Tahura (2018), p. 37.
[11] Şimşek and Bölten (2015), p.1.
[12] McGuinness (2016), p. 13.
[13] Uwazie (2011), p. 13.
[14] Engel and Korf (2005), p. 2.
[15] Engel and Korf (2005), p. 2.
[16] Uwazie (2011), p. 3.
[17] Sandu (2018), p. 103.
[18] Uwazie (2011), p. 3.
[19] Alternative Dispute Resolution Practitioners Guide https://www.usaid.gov/sites/default/files/documents/1868/200sbe.pdf (accessed 7 June 2022).
[20] Bennett (2011), p. 35.
[21] Bilali and Mahmoud (2017), p. 90.
[22] Bilali and Mahmoud (2017), p. 90.

recovering from trauma facilitates reconciliation.[23] The notion of reconciliation and ubuntu are often interlinked.[24] Ubuntu's most notable involvement has been in the field of law.[25] The Interim Constitution was not only the first government document to utilise an African term, but it also laid the groundwork for a new South African society.[26] As a result, the "single word ubuntu" served as a portal for African concepts and ideals to infiltrate South African law.[27] In *Albutt v Centre for the Study of Violence and Reconciliation, and Others*, Froneman J commented that despite appearing to be a fresh concept, South Africa's participatory democracy was based on a historic tenet of traditional African governance.[28]

In 2002 Dino Kritsiotis wrote an article where he highlights how the international community's power could've ended the blight that was then an ongoing conflict in the Democratic Republic of Congo.[29] Africa is a scar on the world's conscience, and if the international community focused on it, this could be healed.[30] Because the selfinterests and mutual interests are now inextricably linked together, the subject of community has become a lesson internationally.[31] Ultimately, the approach to alternative dispute resolution in Africa is community-based and aims to resolve disputes in a manner that is mutually beneficial (mediation and conciliation particularly).[32] When it comes to promoting reconciliation on a global scale, attention needs to be placed on alternative dispute resolution remedies that employ reconciliation as a foundation, such as mediation and conciliation in particular. Interventions in social reconciliation are specifically designed to promote "intergroup understanding", develop "non-violent conflict resolution systems", and heal war wounds.[33] They are distinct from traditional projects and programs in that their major goal is to foster social reconciliation rather than providing services or advancing economic, "social, or political development."[34]

In 1947, peace committees in India's main towns attempted to contain the interethnic strife that was engulfing the country at the time.[35] The committees were

[23] Bilali and Mahmoud (2017), p. 90.

[24] Bennett (2011), p. 33.

[25] Bennett (2011), p. 32.

[26] Bennett (2011), p. 32.

[27] Bennett (2011), p. 30.

[28] *Albutt v Centre for the Study of Violence and Reconciliation* 2010 (3) SA 293 (CC) para 90 accessed in TW Bennett (2011), p. 32.

[29] Kritsiotis (2002), p. 969.

[30] Kritsiotis (2002), p. 969.

[31] Kritsiotis (2002), p. 969.

[32] Alternative Dispute Resolution and Facilitative Process https://www.bbplaw.attorney/dispute-resolution/ (accessed 9 June 2022).

[33] Kumar (1999), p. 2.

[34] Kumar (1999), p. 2.

[35] Kumar (1999), p. 5.

instrumental in bringing the dispute to a close and restoring peace.[36] Peace committees were recognised for lowering conflict and developing mutual understanding in Nicaragua and South Africa.[37] "In recent years", there has been more discussion on reconciliation as a post-war approach to avoid further conflict.[38] Following the landmark work of South Africa's "Truth and Reconciliation Commission", post-conflict peace-building discourse and practice have increasingly emphasised reconciliation.[39] Alternative dispute resolution on a global scale, similar to how mediation and conciliation are frequently used to improve communications between parties, to "reorient the parties to each other", and develop future-oriented solutions to broadly defined conflicts, could be used to facilitate post-war communication.[40] The African continent has established that alternative dispute resolution is well-suited to traditional African justice ideals, notably the essential value of reconciliation.[41] Furthermore, revolutionary alternative dispute resolution efforts in Ghana, Ethiopia, and Nigeria have yielded significant outcomes, demonstrating the appropriateness of alternative dispute resolution in African environments.[42]

Regional and International arbitration centres in Africa.

In Africa, arbitration is the most widely employed technique of dispute resolution.[43]

Despite the fact that arbitration is a regular technique of "dispute resolution for African parties", the bulk of international arbitrations were previously settled outside of Africa.[44] According to Dr. Muigua, when it comes to international commercial arbitration, Africa as a continent has lagged behind the rest of the globe.[45] Previously, international arbitration centres outside of Africa have led international arbitration concerning African participants.[46] The reasons for this are varied, but they are almost definitely based on the fact that most of these cases include international parties who believe arbitral centres outside of Africa are safer and have more local support.[47]

Africa is a developing continent, and countries like South Africa, Kenya, Mauritius, and Egypt are working to establish themselves as significant participants in the

[36] Kumar (1999), p. 5.

[37] Kumar (1999), p. 5.

[38] Kumar (1999), p. 5.

[39] Brounéus (2007), p. 5.

[40] Menkel-Meadow (2015), p. 8.

[41] Uwazie (2011), p.3.

[42] Uwazie (2011), p. 3.

[43] Kane (2019).

[44] Kane (2019).

[45] Muigua (2016), p. 2.

[46] Kane (2019).

[47] Kane (2019).

arbitration arena.[48] There are over 200 arbitration institutes around the world.[49] The Arbitration Foundation of Southern Africa (hereinafter referred to as 'AFSA') appears to be the premier arbitration centre in Africa in terms of experience, administering arbitration cases under its arbitration rules, with the Cairo Regional Centre for International Commercial Arbitration (hereinafter referred to as 'CRCICA') coming in second, while in terms of "ad hoc arbitration" cases, International Centre for Arbitration and Mediation Abuja (hereinafter referred to as 'ICAMA') is the leading arbitration centre.[50] AFSA has grown significantly over a period of time, and the number of international disputes referred to AFSA has increased significantly.[51] Only ten international conflicts were sent to AFSA for arbitration between 2007 and 2016, in comparison to the "18 referrals it received in 2018."[5252] The amount of "international arbitration referrals" continues to rise.[53] South Africa has established that the country is a force to be reckoned with in terms of international arbitration by being able to draw a large increase in desire for international arbitration in a relatively short period of time after aligning its international arbitration legislation with that of other jurisdictions around the world.[54]

Amongst other African countries, Kenya has put itself on the map in terms of recognisable international arbitration centres.[55] Nairobi Centre for International Arbitration (hereinafter referred to as 'NCIA') was recently introduced as an international arbitral institution in the African region and is based in Nairobi, Kenya.[56] However, the Centre still has a long way to go in terms of effectively carrying out most of its statutory responsibilities.[57] In 2015, however, despite the fact that arbitration was well-established in Southern African, Western, and Central African countries, it had only recently begun to take root in East African jurisdictions such as Kenya.[58] There are various obstacles that Kenya will have to overcome in order to

[48] Herbert Smith Freehills (2017), p. 3.

[49] Mistelis (2004), p. 528.

[50] Onyema (2020).

[51] South Africa is making up for lost time as a competitive international arbitration centre https://www.polity.org.za/article/sa-is-catching-up-fast-as-an-international-arbitration-centre-2020-10-14 (accessed 14 June 2022).

[52] South Africa is making up for lost time as a competitive international arbitration centre https://www.polity.org.za/article/sa-is-catching-up-fast-as-an-international-arbitration-centre-2020-10-14 (accessed 14 June 2022).

[53] South Africa is making up for lost time as a competitive international arbitration centre https://www.polity.org.za/article/sa-is-catching-up-fast-as-an-international-arbitration-centre-2020-10-14 (accessed 14 June 2022).

[54] South Africa is making up for lost time as a competitive international arbitration centre https://www.polity.org.za/article/sa-is-catching-up-fast-as-an-international-arbitration-centre-2020-10-14 (accessed 14 June 2022).

[55] Muigua (2015), p. 7.

[56] Muigua and Maina (2016), p. 4.

[57] Muigua and Maina (2016), p. 5.

[58] Prelogar (2022), p. 529.

establish itself as one of the world's most successful arbitration centres.[59] The success of Kenya's international arbitration institution is largely dependent on its ability to recruit foreign parties and develop trust in its legal infrastructure and jurisdictions.[60] As a result, the NCIA must rise to the occasion and aggressively fulfil its expected role in promoting Kenya as a favoured venue for international arbitration.[61] It must ensure that its national legal system supports international arbitration.[62] The NCIA has the capacity to fulfil all of its legal requirements and perhaps exceed expectations in order to become one of the world's most prestigious international arbitral institutions.[63] Furthermore, using the Mauritius International Arbitration Centre (hereinafter referred to as 'MIAC') in combination with the London Court of International Arbitrations (hereinafter referred to as 'LCIA') to have a credible foundation of what makes a successful international arbitration institution.[64] African states should focus their efforts on contesting the international system's underlying regulatory principles.[65]

The Mauritius Chamber of Commerce and Industry's (hereinafter referred to as 'MCCI') Mediation and Arbitration Center (hereinafter referred to as 'MARC"') is also located in Mauritius.[66] The MARC was created to help "local, regional, and international" enterprises.[67] Furthermore, the MARC's arbitration rules are based on the UNCITRAL Model Law.[68] This forum has engaged in cooperation agreements with arbitral institutions around the world, including those in the "United States, Germany, and France", to create a maximum time restriction "of six months" for the resolution of any case.[69] Mauritius is "the only African country" designated as a "safe seat" by the "DELOS Guide to Arbitration Places" since 1 July 2018.[70] Mauritius was regarded as the "rising star of African arbitral tribunals", as jurisdictions made progress on addressing the legislative concerns and logistical challenges.[71]

The LCIA-MIAC was collectively established by "the Mauritian government" and the LCIA in 2011.[72] The LCIA-MIAC may not have handled many conflicts between 2011 and 2018, but it was a welcome regionalisation of arbitration, and it

---

[59] Muyala (2014), p. 28.
[60] Prelogar (2022), p. 529.
[61] Muyala (2014), p. 7.
[62] Muyala (2014), p. 13.
[63] Muyala (2014), p. 18.
[64] Muyala (2014), p. 33.
[65] Muyala (2014), p. 15.
[66] Prelogar (2022), p. 540.
[67] Prelogar (2022), p. 540.
[68] Prelogar (2022), p. 540.
[69] Prelogar (2022), p. 540.
[70] Prelogar (2022), p. 538.
[71] Prelogar (2022), p. 528.
[72] Prelogar (2022), p. 539.

garnered local and international support through arbitration provisions that referenced the institution and its norms.[73] The MIAC held an event to commemorate its relaunch after the institution's joint venture with LCIA was terminated in July 2018.[74] The MIAC intends to be the region's leading dispute resolution centre.[75] In addition, when compared to its foreign competitors, its administrative expenditures and arbitrator fees are relatively low.[76] While familiarity with the MARC structure and procedures certainly won over a significant segment of the local market, it is improbable to also have acquired the same level of traction with foreign practitioners as the former LCIA-MIAC Arbitration Centre.[77]

According to the African Development Bank's "comparative assessment of arbitration institutions" in Mauritius, Côte d'Ivoire, and Egypt, it was concluded that the CRCICA in Egypt:

"Remains one of the best arbitration centres across the African continent and can readily be recommended for use by parties from both the African continent and elsewhere."[78]

From the above, it is evident that CRCICA is currently Africa's "leading arbitration centre", with AFSA in second place.[79] State institutions play a vital role in assisting arbitral centres in establishing themselves as international institutions for settlements "in the region."[80] The help could take the form of supporting or enabling the implementation of "international and domestic arbitral" rulings, along with ensuring "minimal involvement in the process" to secure the trust and confidence of potential users both within and outside the region.[81]

The future of the African continent in international arbitration.

A large number of African countries have taken substantial and positive initiatives to build an international arbitration legal system "that meets international standards".[82] Unfortunately, the same characteristics that contribute to Africa's "poor business environment and lack of competitiveness",[83] trouble the functioning of international arbitration due to issues like "corruption, weak institutions, and inadequate infrastructure."[84] Another factor that results in Africa being considered a weaker competitor in the business environment and the international arbitration

[73] Prelogar (2022), p. 539.
[74] Prelogar (2022), p. 539.
[75] Ofodile (2015), p.38.
[76] Prelogar (2022), p. 527.
[77] Nursimulu and Hornan (2019).
[78] Ofodile (2015), p. 25.
[79] Onyema (2020), p. 13.
[80] Muigua (2016), p. 23.
[81] Muigua (2016), p. 23.
[82] Ofodile (2015), p. 10.
[83] Ofodile (2015), p. 10.
[84] Ofodile (2015), p. 10.

environment is the existence of the bias images created of Africa as a "corrupt" and "uncivilized continent."[85]

Despite the remarkable growth in African states "like Mauritius and Rwanda", many countries, notably Nigeria, the African continent's largest economy, remain among the world's "least competitive economies" and do not always provide a secure and hospitable climate for international arbitration.[86] The use and application of these rules "in managing disputes in Nigeria" has been plagued by distrust caused by pervasive corruption and a "lack of faith in the judicial".[87] Even if one of the parties to an international dispute is a Nigerian, the "international contractual agreements" escape Nigerian law.[88] Though it is still up to the parties in disagreement to decide who will arbitrate their cases, Africans must recognise that Africans are well-versed in the reality of Africans and are thus better equipped to deal with "them not just professionally but also pragmatically."[89] A lesson could be learned from Singapore, where Singaporeans handle half of the arbitral cases heard there.[90] Inter-African and intra-African conflicts should be resolved predominantly by African arbitrators.[91] Although, "the number of African arbitrators" keep increasing and more arbitration cases that involve African parties are heard, the amount of arbitration proceedings conducted in Africa is miserably low, according to the "ICC Dispute Resolution Statistics" (0.001% in 2016).[92] In international disputes, usually, disputing parties prefer to choose "non-nationals as arbitrators", leading to instances in which even Africans prefer non-Africans as arbitrators.[93] As a result, the outside world perceives Africa as a location "where there are no arbitrators" with the knowledge and experience to serve as international arbitrators.[94] Because of cultural disparities, non-African disputants have long been sceptical of African international business arbitrators.[95] These discrepancies could be related to "economic, political, or legal developments", resulting in differing perspectives on topics, "prejudices, and conflicts of interest", particularly in international commercial connections.[96] Africa must use competent arbitration institutions on the continent as well as internationally, to foster the growth and development of arbitration jurisprudence and knowledge, making African countries more competitive in the global arbitration

[85] Muigua (2016), p. 14.
[86] Ofodile (2015), p. 43.
[87] Abe (2013), p. 147.
[88] Abe (2013), p.147.
[89] Nkusi (2018).
[90] Nkusi (2018)
[91] Nkusi (2018)
[92] Olugbemi and Adebanjo (2020).
[93] Muigua (2016), p. 17.
[94] Muigua (2016), p. 18.
[95] Muigua (2016), p. 6.
[96] Muigua (2016), p. 6.

market.[97] Countries with much more evolved arbitration systems should collaborate with African arbitration systems that are just getting started to train and teach arbitrators.[98] Despite the fact that the continent now has a big number of qualified arbitrators, the majority of whom come from Nigeria in West Africa, "there is a need" to teach "even more arbitrators" in order to serve the region's enormous population.[99] Training, seminars, workshops, and other events organised by nations with more evolved arbitration systems which will give African arbitrators more exposure to arbitration information, which will lead to the future growth "of home-grown arbitration in Africa."[100] It is necessary to dispel the old anxieties produced "by Western countries" and "their trading entities", which must be dispelled as current commercial realities emerge.[101101] All major Western countries have virtually completely changed their arbitral legislation.[102] However, in many African countries, the legislation is still in the same obsolete form as when it was imported.[103] African countries are rightly concerned about the overwhelming dominance of multinational firms with financial resources considerably exceeding their own and tentacles extending into other countries.[104] African governments and businesspeople must also make more use of these arbitration mechanisms "in the resolution of inter-state" conflicts as well as disputes with foreigners.[105] Arbitration will continue to increase due to the reasons stated above, as well as the complexity and experience of African arbitration centres in significant jurisdictions such as Kenya, Mauritius, South Africa and Nigeria.[106] Because of the well-established link between commercial development and African professionals, there is a growing drive for commercial conflicts to be settled on the continent, rather than being 'exported' to international centres like London and Paris.[107] Positive action by African countries, such as revising legislation and establishing and strengthening international arbitration institutions, would, in turn, ensure that the popularity of international arbitrations held in Africa continues to rise.[108]

Referring African issues to European arbitral authorities for resolution is both expensive and ineffective.[109] Arbitration between African parties, on the other hand, is becoming more common, and a number of governments have built high-quality

[97] Onyema (2008), p. 1.

[98] Olugbemi and Adebanjo (2020).

[99] Olugbemi and Adebanjo (2020).

[100] Olugbemi and Adebanjo (2020).

[101] Sempasa (1992), p. 397.

[102] Sempasa (1992), p. 391.

[103] Sempasa (1992), p. 391.

[104] Sempasa (1992), p. 393.

[105] Sempasa (1992), p. 397.

[106] Kane (2019).

[107] Kane (2019).

[108] Muyala (2014), p. 13.

[109] Muigua (2016), p. 3.

dispute resolution centres and focused attention on modifications to local laws to encourage the process.[110] The growing importance of arbitration as a form of "alternative dispute resolution in Africa" is evidenced by the growth of arbitration centres throughout the continent.[111] The judiciary supports this since it can assist in reducing the backlog in the judicial system.[112] African countries are beginning to recognise the value of arbitration in promoting economic development,[113] which can be deduced from the establishment of NCIA by "the Kenyan government" promoting the capital city as a regional financial centre.[114] International commercial arbitration, when used effectively and consistently, has the ability to stimulate investors to do business with confidence, trusting that their problems would be resolved quickly.[115] This may increase users' trust in African arbitral institutions, reawakening the continent's otherwise dormant arbitral institutions and arbitration practice.[116] Dr. Muigua declares that there is reason to be optimistic about the future and that Africa's arbitration institutions and practices have the ability to expand and prosper.[117]

7.2 Conclusion

Based on the number of arbitration institutions that have been founded in Africa, it may be concluded that the continent has emerged as a major player in international arbitration. Although Africa already has the capacity to be called a "competitor" in the international arbitration arena, there is still room for progress, and Africa has the ability to lead 1 day. Furthermore, based on its assessment of reconciliation as a foundation for mediation and conciliation, Africa has demonstrated how its approach to ensuring reconciliation on the continent can help the rest of the world understand that it is not about winning, but about the process of reconciling.

[110] Muigua (2016), p. 4.
[111] Muigua (2016), p. 24.
[112] Ofodile (2015), p. 51.
[113] Muigua (2016), p. 23.
[114] Ostrove (2018).
[115] Muigua (2016), p. 24.
[116] Muigua (2016), p. 24.
[117] Muigua (2016), p. 24.

References

Abe OO (2013) The legal framework for the institutionalisation of international commercial arbitration in Nigeria: a critical review. Afe Babalola University: J Sustain Dev Law Policy 1 (1):132

Bennett TW (2011) Ubuntu: an African equity. Potchefstroom Electric Law J 14(4):30

Bilali R, Mahmoud R (2017) Confronting history and reconciliation: a review of civil society's approaches to transforming conflict narratives. In: Psaltis C et al (eds) History education and conflict transformation, p 77

Brounéus K (2007) Reconciliation and development

Engel A, Korf B (2005) Negotiation and mediation techniques for natural resource management, vol 3. Food and Agriculture Organization of the United Nations, Rome, p 1

Friedman LM (1989) Litigation and society. Annu Rev Sociol 15:1

Kane G (2019) Africa: a bright future for dispute resolution. https://www.webberwentzel.com/News/Documents/2019/23-05-2019-africa-a-bright-future-for-disputeresolution.pdf?utm_content=1558621195&utm_medium=social&utm_source=linkedin. Accessed 12 June 2022

Kritsiotis D (2002) Imagining the international community. EJIL 13(4):961

Kumar K (1999) Promoting social reconciliation in post-conflict societies. United States Agency Int Dev 24:2

McGuinness HMJC (2016) Alternative dispute resolution-mediation and conciliation

Menkel-Meadow C (2015) Mediation, arbitration, and alternative dispute resolution. International encyclopedia of the social and behavioral sciences, Elsevier Ltd 59:8

Mistelis L (2004) International arbitration-corporate attitudes and practices-12 perceptions tested: myths, data and analysis rese. Am Rev Int Arbitr 15:525

Muigua K (2016) Promoting international commercial arbitration in Africa. Alternative dispute resolution

Muigua K, Maina J (2016) Effective management of commercial disputes: opportunities for the Nairobi centre for international arbitration. Am Rev Int Arbitr

Muyala MIW (2014) The effectiveness of an arbitration institution is seen to be determined by a number of factors, ranging from its pricing strategy to the overall strength of the host state's legal system, LL.M Dissertation, University of Nairobi 1

Nkusi FK (2018) Whose responsibility is it to scale up arbitration in Africa? https://www.tralac.org/news/article/13013-whose-responsibility-is-it-to-scale-up-arbitration-in-africa.html. Accessed 1 8 June 2022

Nursimulu B, Hornan B (2019) The choice of a Mauritian arbitral institution http://arbitrationblog.kluwerarbitration.com/2019/12/23/the-choice-of-a-mauritian-arbitral-institution/. Accessed 13 June 2022

Ofodile UE (2015) Africa and international: from accommodation and acceptance to active engagement. Transnational Dispute Manag 12(4):1

Olugbemi AO, Adebanjo T (2020) Improving homegrown international arbitration in Africa. https://papers.ssrn.com/sol3/papers.cfm?abstract_id=3636943. Accessed 18 June 2022

Onyema E (2020) Arbitration in Africa survey report: 2020 Top African arbitral centres and seats

Ostrove M (2018) Developments in African arbitration. https://globalarbitrationreview.com/review/the-middle-eastern-and-african-arbitrationreview/2018/article/developments-in-african-arbitration. Accessed 18 June 2022

Prelogar JB (2022) From forecast to five-cast: the arbitral promise of Africa. University of Pennsylvania, J Int Law 43(2):523

Sandu C (2018) Romania: traditional conflict resolution mechanisms used by the Roma communities. Conflict Stud Q 22:95

Sempasa SL (1992) Obstacles to international commercial arbitration in African countries. Int & Comparative Law Q 41(2):387

Şimşek PANS, Bölten AK (2015) General overview as to the distinction between litigation and alternative dispute resolution methods
Tahura U (2018) Will ADR be able to impact on access to justice and litigation costs? In: 2018 ALSA conference law in the Asian century
Uwazie EE (2011) Alternative dispute resolution in Africa: preventing conflict and enhancing stability. Washington DC Africa: Centre for Strategic Studies 16:1

Chane Williamson a vibrant individual whose life is a colourful tapestry woven with a love for food and adventure. She holds an LLB and LLM from the University of Pretoria. Education stands at the forefront of her passions, viewing it not only as a pathway to personal success but as a powerful tool to break barriers. She is in the process of navigating the world of academia with enthusiasm, recognizing the transformative impact it can have on shaping one's destiny. Beyond the books, as she relishes in culinary adventures, board games, and the thrill of outdoor experiences. Her time at Madelief, the university residence, played a pivotal role in shaping not only her academic trajectory but also in contributing to the dynamic powerhouse that she is evolving into.

Chapter 8
A Comparative Study of Nigeria and South Africa's from an Enforcement Perspective

Okadazim Makinde and Rashri Baboolal-Frank

8.1 Introduction

As earlier mentioned, the parties in any arbitration process assume that, unless a settlement is made along the way, the procedures will conclude with an award and that the opposing party will comply with the award.[1] An unsatisfied party to the proceedings may appeal an arbitral award, making it harder for the successful party to enforce it.[2] However, questions about the appropriateness or otherwise of challenging and enforcing an arbitral award continue to elicit a wide range of comments.[3]

While it is difficult to generalize the difficulties in recognizing and enforcing arbitral awards across the region, it is arguably a common theme that the difficulties stem from the various levels of development of arbitration regimes in the various unharmonized African countries. Where similar regimes exist, local courts' decisions on the recognition and enforceability of arbitral awards may differ.[4]

The goal of this chapter is to compare the Nigerian and South African positions on the enforcement of arbitration awards by examining the various applicable mechanisms in light of their unique characteristics, strengths, and weaknesses.

This chapter is based on the chapter 4 of ON Makinde LLM research dissertation available on the UP Law repository.

[1] Blackaby et al. (2009), p. 513.

[2] Eyongndi and Ojuade (2019), pp. 29–37.

[3] Adedoyin (2022).

[4] Abdallah and Esmail (2021).

O. Makinde (✉) · R. Baboolal-Frank
University of Pretoria, Department of Procedural Law, Faculty of Law, Pretoria, South Africa
e-mail: rashri.baboolal@up.ac.za; rashri.baboolal@up.ac.za

R. Baboolal Frank (ed.), *Dispute Resolution within Africa*,
https://doi.org/10.1007/978-3-031-76261-1_8

8.2 Legal Framework for Recognition and Enforcement of Arbitral Awards

One of the most influential factors that make arbitration appealing in any jurisdiction is a strong legislative framework. The legal system of the arbitration state has a significant impact on the arbitration process.[5] Provisions for the recognition and enforcement of arbitral awards are made under local and international instruments in Nigeria and South Africa. While these instruments facilitate the smooth enforcement of awards in some ways, the process is sometimes hampered in other ways by flaws in these laws.[6]

8.2.1 Enforcement Statutes

The legal systems of African countries differ in many ways. The difficulty in navigating these differences is heightened by the lack of regional harmonisation of laws and policies, as well as a general tendency toward dynamism in the socio-political landscape, which may affect the effectiveness of judicial processes and enforcement.[7]

In Nigeria, the Arbitration and Conciliation Act is the applicable procedural statute for the recognition and enforcement of arbitral awards.[8] Apart from the arbitration statutes which provide for the enforcement of arbitral awards, foreign arbitral awards are also enforceable by registration under statutes dealing with the enforcement of judgments, as judgments are defined as including arbitral awards.[9] The statutes include the Reciprocal Enforcement of Judgements Ordinance 1922 (REJO) and the Foreign Judgments (Reciprocal Enforcement) Act of 1960 (FJREA).[10] An award made by the International Centre for Settlement of Investment Disputes (ICSID) is enforceable in Nigeria under the ICSID (Enforcement of Awards) Act.[11]

The New York Convention applies to any award made in Nigeria or any contracting state where recognition and enforcement of any award arising out of international commercial arbitration are sought under the ACA.[12] However, the

---

[5] Loukas (2016), p. 1.

[6] Moneke (2018), p. 3.

[7] Safeez-Naaz (2019).

[8] Elias, Ijaodola, Oyekan and Ibekwe.

[9] Rhodes-Vivour (2021).

[10] Rhodes-Vivour (2015), p. 544. See also Order 52 Rule 17 of the Federal High Court Civil Procedure Rules, Order 19 Rule 14 of the Federal Capital Territory High Court Rules.

[11] Elias et al. (2022).

[12] Section 54 (1) of the ACA.

contracting state must have reciprocal legislation recognizing the enforcement of arbitral awards made in Nigeria following the Convention's provisions.[13]

Domestic arbitral awards in South Africa can only be recognized and enforced under the Arbitration Act.[14] The International Arbitration Act establishes a legal framework in South Africa for the regulation and enforcement of foreign arbitral awards.[15] The International Arbitration Act also incorporates the UNCITRAL Model Law and the New York Convention into South African law, with minor modifications and adaptations.[16]

8.2.2 *The Issue of Time Limitation*

The time limit within which an award creditor may enforce an arbitral award varies by jurisdiction; there is no uniform regulation on the subject. There is considerable variation in when the time begins to run, in addition to differences in the length of the period. There are also significant differences between limitation period provisions that are expressly applicable or commonly applied to the enforcement of arbitral awards.[17]

The beginning of the limitation period for the enforcement of arbitral awards in Nigeria has been a source of considerable concern.[18] The ACA, for example, does not specify a time limit for filing a court action to enforce arbitration awards, and reliance on federal and state limitation laws may sometimes result in an award creditor not receiving the expected result.[19]

The Limitation Act and the Foreign Judgements (Reciprocal Enforcement) Act are the applicable laws in Nigeria for the limitation of action and the enforcement of awards.[20] States in Nigeria have also enacted legislation on the limitation of action. As a result, the various states' limitation laws are used to determine the time limit for the enforcement of arbitral awards in Nigeria. The time limit will thus be determined by the statute of limitations in each jurisdiction (state) where an arbitral award is sought to be enforced.[21]

[13] Mordi et al. (2022)

[14] Section 31 of the Arbitration Act 42 of 1965.

[15] Section 16 of the International Arbitration Act 15 of 2017.

[16] Smith (2021).

[17] Stier (2021).

[18] Akoni (2022), p. 1.

[19] Azikiwe and Onyia (2019).

[20] Cap. 522, Laws of the Federation of Nigeria, 2004, Cap F35, Laws of the Federation of Nigeria, 2004.

[21] Awoyale (2019), p. 92 Section 52 and 8(1)(d) of the Limitation laws Cap L84 of Lagos State 2015, Section 7(1)(d) of the Limitation Law of the Federal Capital Territory Abuja, Section 4(1)(c) and Section 4(1)(c) and 18 of the Limitation Law of Benue State 1988, Section 34 and 16 of the Limitation Law of Rivers State 1988, Section 18 of the Limitation Law of Bauchi State 1991.

It should be noted that, while the majority of these state laws make no mention of their applicability to the enforcement of arbitral awards, they do refer to contractual actions. However, because arbitration is a contract in and of itself, and because it is made a court order, it is enforced as a court judgment, making the provisions of the law applicable to the enforcement of arbitral awards.[22] In this regard, the enforcement mechanism available for judgments obtained through civil proceedings is equally applicable to arbitral awards obtained through any applicable legislation.[23]

After an award is made, there are no statutory time limits in South Africa under the Arbitration Act and the IAA,[24] which provide the statutory framework for the enforcement of domestic and foreign arbitral awards, respectively.[25] The Constitutional Court has held and subsequently confirmed, that the Prescription Act,[26] which provides for the limitation of periods, does not apply to employment law arbitral awards rendered by arbitration tribunals.[27] The Supreme Court of Appeal added to the finality of this issue by generalizing all arbitral awards as not constituting a debt and thus not subject to the Prescription Act's limitation period.[28]

8.2.3 Jurisdiction of the Enforcing Court

In Nigeria and South Africa, the approach to the recognition and enforcement of arbitral awards is generally consistent, though each country requires that an application for recognition and enforcement of the award be made to the relevant domestic court with jurisdiction over the particular arbitral award.[29] It is, however, prudent to seek recognition and enforcement of an arbitral award in the specific court that would have had jurisdiction over the subject matter of the dispute resolved in arbitration.[30]

The competent authority in Nigeria to recognize and enforce an arbitral award is determined by the statute under which the application is made. The Federal High Court and the various State High Courts are the competent courts with jurisdiction to recognize and enforce arbitral awards, whether domestic or foreign, under the

[22] Awoyale (2019), p. 195.

[23] Adaralegbe (2006).

[24] Arbitration Act 42 of 1965 and The International Arbitration Act 15 of 2017.

[25] Fletcher and De-Waal (2022).

[26] Act 69 of 1969. 'Under section 11 of the Prescription Act, Arbitration Awards are treated as debts. Where the award is made an order of the court, it expires after thirty (30) years but where not made an order of court expires after three (3) years.

[27] Mogaila V. Coca-Cola Fortune (Pty) Ltd 2018 1 SA.

[28] Brompton Court Body Corporate V. Khumalo (398/2017) 2018 ZASCA 27.

[29] Lafleur (2021).

[30] Kabo Air Limited V. The O' Corporation Limited (2014) LPELR 23616.

Arbitration and Conciliation Act.[31] The supreme court has resolved the major question of whether both courts have concurrent jurisdiction over the same matter.[32]

It is recommended, however, that a party seeking to enforce an arbitral award in Nigeria under the ACA approach the Federal High Court because it has federal jurisdiction, which means that an execution order against the award debtor's assets can be enforced in any state of the Federation.[33] The territorial restrictions that apply to state high courts do not apply to the Federal High Court, making the execution process less burdensome.[34]

The Supreme Court of Nigeria has original jurisdiction to hear ICSID enforcement proceedings.[35] This is possibly the quickest procedure in Nigeria for enforcing an arbitral award because there is little or no room for objections to the award's enforcement.[36] These types of awards are not covered by the ACA.

Generally, an arbitration award is not automatically enforced under South African arbitration laws unless it is first recognized and made an order of the court.[37] A court with jurisdiction to recognize or enforce arbitral awards is defined in the Arbitration Act as "any court of a provincial or local division of the Supreme Court of South Africa having jurisdiction."[38]

Even though it is not expressly stated, practice over the years has shown that arbitral awards in South Africa have been enforced through application/motion proceedings in the high court[39] and the motion court.[40] As a result, once the arbitral award is made a court order, it takes on the status of any court judgment or award and can be enforced in the same manner as described above in the Arbitration Act.[41]

---

[31] SPA Ajibade & Co. 'Challenging and Enforcing Arbitration Awards in Nigeria' https://spaajibade.com/challenging-and-enforcing-arbitration-awards-in-nigeria/. (Accessed 24 August 2022) and Section 57 of the ACA.

[32] Adeoye Magbagbeola V. Temitope Sanni (2002) 4 NWLR (Pt 756) 193.... The Court held that the definition of "high court" under the Arbitration and Conciliation Act is applicable to arbitral proceedings. They referred to Section 57(1) which defines "court" as the High Court of a State, the Federal Capital Territory or the Federal High Court and a "judge" as any judge of such courts'.

[33] Ahaji Albishir & Sons Ltd. V. Bayero University, Kano (1996) LPELR-13928.

[34] Ayeni (2022).

[35] Section 1 of the ICSID Act, Cap 120, Laws of the Federation of Nigeria, 2004.

[36] Okoronkwo (2022).

[37] Section 31 of the Arbitration Act 42 of 1965 & Section 16(3) of the International Arbitration Act.

[38] Section 1 of the Arbitration Act 42 of 1965.

[39] Holloway and October (2015).

[40] Rule 6(5)(a) of the Uniform Rules of Court.

[41] Fletcher and De-Waal (2022).

8.2.4 Vagueness of the Term Public Policy

The concept of public policy is so broad that it may appear difficult to distinguish what is and is not a matter of public policy.[42] The international community has expressed concern that the ambiguity of the term Public Policy allows states to refuse recognition and enforcement of arbitral awards on regional and possibly unexpected grounds when it suits them.[43] Public policy has been described as multifaceted, open-textured, and flexible, with many guises and thus a wide range of vocabulary and ambiguities. Legislators and courts are understandably hesitant to describe public policy in detail.[44]

Domestic and international elements are included in public policy. On the one hand, public policy operates entirely within a domestic relationship, but when applied to international arbitration, it serves as a constraint on foreign law's access to the domestic system.[45] Public policy is also one of the irregularities listed by the New York Convention as grounds for refusing to enforce arbitral awards. It allows national courts to refuse to enforce an award that contradicts fundamental principles of the forum state's legal system.[46]

In comparison to all other grounds for refusing enforcement of foreign arbitral awards, the public policy ground is highly vulnerable to abuse due to its imprecise definition and the fact that what constitutes public policy varies from country to country. The meaning of public policy in the enforcement of arbitral awards is heavily dependent on the court's interpretation of what constitutes public policy.[47]

The term "public policy" is not defined in the ACA or other statutes governing the enforcement of arbitral awards in Nigeria.[48] However, the courts in Nigeria have attempted to define the concept of public policy.[49] The court where recognition or enforcement of an award is sought may, regardless of the country in which the award

---

[42] Kleiman and Pauly (2019).

[43] Ostrove et al. (2021).

[44] Cole (1985), p. 366.

[45] Sammartano (2014), p. 506.

[46] Tosun (2019).

[47] Emelonye and Emelonye (2021), p. 276.

[48] Nwakoby and Aduaka (2015), p. 123.

[49] In Macaulay V. FZB of Austria (1999) 4 NWLR (Pt 600) 599 the Court defined public policy as principles under which the freedom of contract and private dealings is restricted by law for the good of the community.

Also, in Dale Power Systems Plc V. Witt & Busch Ltd (2001) 8 NWLR (Pt 716) 699 the Court of Appeal defined a public policy to mean community sense and common conscience extended and applied throughout the state to matters of public morals, health, safety, welfare and the like.

The Supreme Court in Okonkwo V. Okagbue (1994) 9 NWLR (Pt 368) 301 also defined 'public policy' as "the ideals which for the time being prevail in any community a to the conditions necessary to ensure its welfare, so that anything is treated as against public policy if it is generally injurious to the public interest."

is made, refuse to recognize or enforce that award if the court determines that such recognition or enforcement is contrary to Nigerian public policy.[50]

In enforcing or refusing awards, Nigerian courts typically take a conservative approach to the application of public policy.[51] The Nigerian Courts will almost certainly only find that an arbitral award (particularly a foreign arbitral award) is contrary to public policy in Nigeria, that the award is of such a nature that it causes a glaring inconsistency with Nigerian law, or that enforcing the award would violate the very fabric of the Nigerian legal system.[52]

South African public policy applies to both domestic and foreign awards, so the court does not approach the issue differently.[53] In South Africa, the question of public policy has been whether the courts will follow the dictates of domestic law as guided by the constitution or follow the international trend.[54] There is little certainty about how South African courts will approach the enforcement of international awards. Public policy is a matter of fact, not law, and it evolves in response to "the general sense of the community, good morals, manifested in public opinion."[55]

Although there is no agreed definition of public policy in South Africa, it has been suggested that when considering the enforcement of arbitral awards, public policy should be construed narrowly and limited to violations of fundamental principles of justice or morality.[56] In a few cases, South African courts considered the public policy exception to the enforcement of foreign and/or domestic arbitral awards.[57] In those cases, the court considered whether the party opposing enforcement could successfully invoke the public policy defence.[58]

In South Africa, it is the responsibility of the courts to determine what is meant by the term "public policy" or what is considered to be against good morals in any given case, and such power should not be exercised hastily or rashly. It should be used sparingly and only in the clearest of cases, lest arbitrary and indiscriminate use of the power results in uncertainty about the validity of contracts. This is especially true

---

[50] Section 52(2)(b)(ii) and Section 48(c) of the ACA.

[51] Eme (2021).

[52] Abiru (2020).

[53] Holloway and October (2015).

[54] Lane (2019).

[55] Amod V. Multilateral Motor Vehicle Accident Fund (1999) 1 SA 319.

[56] Kahn (1977), pp. 564, 570.

[57] Gutsche Family Investments (Pty) Ltd and Others v Mattia Equity Group (Pty) Ltd and Others 2007 5 SA 491; Seton Co v Silveroak Industries Ltd. 2000 2 SA 215; Telcordia Technologies Inc. v Telkom SA Ltd. 2007 3 SA 266 (SCA).

In the Seton company case, the court held that .... 'The court will refuse to recognise an arbitral award, where on the face of the award and the arbitration agreement it is clear that the award is contrary to public policy without the need to consider extraneous evidence, for example where it is clear that the arbitration was based on an illegal contract'.

[58] Robertson (2011), p. 14.

when individual judges attempt to apply their perceptions of the moral sense of the community.[59]

While it may take some time for a foreign arbitral award to be made an order of a South African court, parties can be confident that South African courts will continue to uphold public policy principles while remaining practical and impartial when deciding to recognize and enforce a foreign arbitral award.[60]

8.2.5 Provisions of the Grounds for Setting Aside Arbitral Awards

Sections 29 and 30 of the ACA outline the very limited grounds on which a court in Nigeria can vacate an arbitral award at the request of an aggrieved award debtor.[61] due to its open-ended effect,[62] it allows a party to challenge an arbitral tribunal's award on grounds of misconduct.[63] The crux of the issue is defining what constitutes misconduct on the part of the arbitrator, as the courts have always given this matter a wide interpretation.[64]

The term misconduct, for example, is not defined in the ACA, and as a result of this omission, Nigerian courts have resorted to several definitions.[65] The Supreme Court in the case of held Taylor Woodrow Nig. Ltd. V. Suddeutsche Etna-Werk Gmbh held thus

> It is difficult to give an exhaustive definition of what may amount to misconduct on the part of an arbitrator or umpire. The expression is of wide import, for an arbitrator's award, unless set aside, entitles the beneficiary to call on the executive power of the state to enforce it, and it is the court's function to ensure that the executive power of the court is not abused. It is accordingly misconduct for an arbitrator to fail to comply with the terms, express or implied, of the arbitration agreement. But even if the arbitrator fully complies with those terms, he will be guilty of misconduct if he makes an award which on grounds of public policy ought not to be enforced. Much confusion has been caused by the fact that the expression 'misconduct' is used to describe both these quite separate grounds for setting aside an award, and it is not wholly clear in some of the decided cases on which of these two grounds the award has been set aside. However, on one or other of these grounds the expression includes on the one hand that which is misconduct by any standard, such as being bribed or

59 Sasfin (Pty) Ltd V. Beukes [1989] 1 All SA 347 (A) at 350–352.

60 Balusik (2019) http://arbitrationblog.kluwerarbitration.com/2019/02/17/the-know-how-to-enforcing-foreign-arbitration-awards-in-south-africa/.

61 Nwakoby (2010), p. 3.

62 The Court may set aside an arbitral award pursuant to Section 30(1) of the ACA 'Where an arbitrator has misconducted himself, or where the arbitral proceedings have been improperly procured.

63 Akanbi (2012), p. 325.

64 Baker Marine Nig. Ltd. V. Chevron Nig. Ltd. (2000) 12 NWLR (Pt 681) 404. Para. 5. Lists over 100 forms of conduct which may constitute misconduct by an arbitrator.

65 Taylor Woodrow Nig. Ltd. V. Suddeutsche Etna-Werk Gmbh (1993) 4 NWLR (Pt 285) 127).

> corrupted, and on the other hand mere 'technical' misconduct, such as making a mere mistake as to the scope of the authority conferred by the agreement of reference. That does not mean that every irregularity of procedure amounts to misconduct.

Since the ACA does not define what constitutes misconduct, parties to arbitral proceedings have frequently used the concept to file frivolous and unfounded allegations and complaints against an arbitrator, stifling the enforcement of awards.[66] Nigerian courts have also become wary of granting such frivolous applications without due and thorough consideration of all the facts before the court.[67]

In South Africa, the problem remains the same in terms of the Arbitration Act's lack of definition of the terms for the ground of setting aside.[68] Even though the guiding principle of consensual arbitration is finality, the arbitration Act and the IAA contain several mechanisms for challenging an arbitral award.[69]

The grounds for setting aside an arbitration award are not simply there for the taking in South Africa.[70] This is due to the omnibus nature of the evidence required to prove these grounds, as there is no specific definition of the terms as stated in the arbitration laws.[71] Parties seeking to resolve disputes through arbitration should keep in mind that an arbitrator's role is to strike a balance between competing issues based on the facts and evidence before them.[72]

8.3 The Judicial System (Court Intervention and Interference)

It is impossible to emphasize enough the importance of an effective judicial system in arbitration, particularly in the enforcement of arbitration awards.[73] A functioning judiciary is an essential component of any civil society.[74] Backlogs, delays, and corruption plague the judiciaries of many African countries, including Nigeria and

---

[66] Guinness Nig. Plc V. Nibol Properties Ltd (2015) 5 CLRN 65, Triana Ltd. V. Universal Trust Bank PLC (2009) 12 NWLR (Pt. 1155) 313.

[67] Arbico Nig. Ltd V. Nigeria Machine Tools Ltd. (2002) 15 NWLR (Pt 1).

[68] Section 33(1) of the Arbitration Act provides that the court can set aside an arbitral award where:

(a) Any member of the arbitration tribunal has misconducted himself in relation to his duties as arbitrator or umpire;
(b) An arbitration tribunal has committed any gross irregularity in the conduct of the arbitration proceedings or has exceeded its powers.

[69] Manko and Arends (2021).

[70] State Information Technology Agency SOC Limited (SITA) V. ELCB Information Services (Pty) Ltd and Another (995/16) 2017 ZASCA 120.

[71] Section 33(1) of the Arbitration Act.

[72] Mpahlwa (2017).

[73] Moneke (2018), p. 4.

[74] Tobi (1997), p. 21.

South Africa thereby making the rapid resolution of disputes is becoming increasingly difficult.[75]

Arbitration's effectiveness as a commercial dispute resolution mechanism is measured by the ease with which the resulting arbitral award is enforced through the courts if the award debtor does not voluntarily comply with the award.[76] The desirability of a jurisdiction as a seat of arbitration is determined by the quality of judicial support and the respect for minimal judicial intervention.[77]

Nigerian courts have generally, particularly in recent times, taken a pro-arbitration stance in deciding arbitration-related cases, including the enforcement of arbitral awards.[78] The case law in Nigeria is replete with examples of Nigerian courts giving effect to the parties' agreement by refusing to consider actions that may interfere with the outcome of the arbitration process.[79] Unfortunately, this is not always the case, as parties continue to file frivolous grounds to challenge unfavourable awards. On these frivolous grounds, Nigerian courts have repeatedly delayed the enforcement of arbitration awards.[80]

The enforcement process is also hampered by the Nigerian courts' slowness in resolving cases.[81] The losing party in arbitration frequently attempts to use the court as a tool to prevent the winning party from benefiting from the arbitration's outcome, usually with no effort made by the court to discourage such antics.[82] Every application to enforce an arbitral award in Nigeria is potentially appealable to the court of first instance, the court of appeal, and the Supreme Court. Due to this difficulty, the enforcement of arbitral awards has continued to drag on for years.[83]

Without a doubt, the right to appeal a High Court decision is protected by the Constitution.[84] Nonetheless, the exercise of this right of appeal appears to mock the nature of arbitration as a final and binding means of resolving disputes. Arbitration, rather than being an alternative to litigation, becomes the first step toward litigation in the end.[85]

---

[75] ObiOkoye (2005), p. 11.

[76] Azikiwe and Onyia (2019).

[77] Aje-Famuyide and Akano (2021), p. 24.

[78] Shasore and Uka (2022).

[79] Metroline (Nig.) Ltd. V. Dikko (2021) 2 NWLR (Pt. 1761) 422, Baker Marine Nigeria Ltd. V. Chevron Nigeria Ltd. (2003) 13 NWLR (Pt. 997) 276.

[80] Limak Yatirim Enerji Uretim Isletme Hizmetleri Ve Insaat A. S. & Ors V. Sahelian Energy and Integrated Services Ltd., ICC Case No. 21617/ZF/AYZ .... The Court of Appeal upheld the decision of the Federal High Court, Abuja, which set aside a final arbitral award published on 28 June 2018 by a Tribunal of the International Chamber of Commerce (ICC) International Court of Arbitration seated in Geneva, Switzerland.

[81] IPCO (Nig.) Ltd. V. Nigerian National Petroleum Corporation Ltd. (2014) ECWH 576, where Gross J. held "...... the mill of justice grinds slowly in Nigeria. In particular, Nigeria is not geared toward arbitration in a manner which meets the international standards it agreed to".

[82] Uba (2017), pp. 12–13.

[83] Adewale and Okpara (2013) https://www.templars-law.com/413-2/.

[84] Section 241 of the Constitution of the Federal Republic of Nigeria, 1999 as amended.

[85] Sundersons Ltd & Anor V. Cruiser Shipping PTE Ltd & Anor (2015) 17 NWLR (Pt 1488) 357.

Even though there have been instances where the court interfered in the enforcement of awards by not considering arbitration awards to be valid,[86] there is virtually no risk of a South African Court intervening to frustrate the enforcement of arbitral awards in South Africa.[87] South African courts have recently expressed strong support for arbitration and the enforcement of arbitration awards.[88] The Supreme Court of Appeal[89] and Constitutional Court[90] decisions recognize the principle of party autonomy[91] and confirm that court intervention in arbitration and the enforcement of arbitral awards should be limited.[92] South African courts regard the principle of party autonomy as a manifestation of the parties' freedom to enter into and carry out private arbitration agreements.[93]

Parties may, however, seek to delay arbitration proceedings and enforcement through frequent court applications; however, due to the court's supportive approach, attempts to delay proceedings through frequent court applications generally fail in South Africa.[94]

8.4 Conversion of Money Award to Local Currency

The award does not need to be converted into local currency in Nigeria. If payment was made in that currency, a court can enter judgment in that currency. A Nigerian court can make a foreign currency award. If the claim was made in a foreign currency and the judgment was also rendered in that currency, execution should also be carried out in that currency.[95] In rare cases and with special permission, an arbitral

[86] Baboolal-Frank (2019), p. 366; Telecordia Technologies Inc. V. Telcom SA Ltd 2007 5 BCLR 503 (SCA).

[87] Williams (2020), p. 14. and Article 5, Schedule 1 of the IAA.

[88] Khum MK Investments and Bie Joint Venture (Pty) Limited V. Escom Holdings SOC and Another (30,169/2018) 2020 ZAGP JHC 7.

[89] Eskom holdings Ltd. V. The Joint Venture of Edison Jehamo (Pty) Ltd. and KEC and KEC International Limited and Others (177/2020) 2021 ZASCA 138.

[90] Myathaza V. Johannesburg Metropolitan Bus Services SOC Limited t/a Metrobus and Others 2018 1 SA 38.

[91] Gao (2021), p. 123.

"The party autonomy principle permits parties to any international commercial agreement to determine which laws apply to their agreement.[2] The party autonomy theory was initially proposed by academics, but now enjoys wide acceptance in domestic law. This principle is recognized on a voluntary basis in many countries. It is forced neither by alliance nor by international bodies. Despite obvious differences in the nature and application of case law and statutes, each nation is impacted in a similar way by the notion of party autonomy since it permits parties to opt for relevant laws when encountering commercial relations."

[92] Kron and Forshaw (2020).

[93] Rajpal et al. (2002).

[94] Williams (2020), p. 14.

[95] Mordi et al. (2022).

award debtor in Nigeria may be allowed to pay the foreign arbitral award debt in local currency. If so, it must be at the current exchange rate on the date of execution.[96]

To be enforceable in South Africa, a foreign arbitral award ordering money to be paid and expressed in a foreign currency must first be converted to rand, the local currency. The award must be made a court order as if it were a payment award in rand, based on the exchange rate at the time of the award, not the date of the order of enforcement.[97]

8.5 Reciprocity

The enforcement of arbitral awards also includes the critical preliminary decision of whether an arbitral award should be classified as a foreign or domestic award. If it qualifies as a foreign award, its recognition and enforcement are subject to different conditions in different countries. The reciprocity of arbitral awards is one such condition.[98]

The reciprocity reservation states that a state may recognize and enforce awards made in another contracting state's territory. The primary goal of the New York Convention is to ensure that contracting states implement both foreign and non-domestic arbitral awards.[99] This provision has a significant impact on the New York Convention and, if states choose, narrows the scope of application.[100]

As a result, these countries will only recognize and enforce Convention awards. This reservation can be interpreted negatively, but there is currently a rapidly growing number of signatories, particularly in Africa, including South Africa and Nigeria.[101]

The UNCITRAL Model Law,[102] which provides universal enforceability of awards, supplements the New York Convention.[103] It requires member states to ensure that such awards are recognized and enforced like domestic awards.[104]

Since the ACA domesticated the New York Convention and the UNCITRAL Model Law foreign arbitral awards can be enforced in Nigeria under the ACA, the New York Convention, or the UNCITRAL Model Law.[105] The ACA ensures that an

[96] Mordi et al. (2022).

[97] Holloway and October (2015).

[98] Szászy (1965), p. 658.

[99] Article II (1) and (3) of the New York Convention.

[100] Becker (2005), p. 9.

[101] Asouzu (2001), p. 188.

[102] Article III of the New York Convention.

[103] Article 35 and 36 of the UNCITRAL Model Law.

[104] Baykitch and Hui (2008), pp. 364–371.

[105] 2nd Schedule of the ACA.

award is recognized regardless of the jurisdiction in which it was granted.[106] The conditionality of reciprocity of arbitral award enforcement is not a requirement for the enforcement of an arbitral award.[107]

As a member state of the Commonwealth of Nations, foreign awards may also be enforced in Nigeria through the Foreign Judgements (Reciprocal Enforcement) Act,[108] which was created to ensure fluidity in the registration and enforcement of court judgments obtained in the United Kingdom, including arbitral awards, so long as the award is enforceable in the country in which the award was handed down. The implication is that awards from countries that do not guarantee substantial reciprocity in the enforcement of Nigerian awards will also be refused enforcement.[109]

South Africa, like Nigeria, has ratified the New York Convention and the UNCITRAL Model Law, and the principles contained therein are incorporated into their national laws. In South Africa, the IAA[110] provides for the recognition and enforcement of arbitration agreements and foreign arbitral awards.

These provisions give effect to South Africa's international law obligations as a New York Convention an UNCITRAL Model Law contracting state.[111] As a result, because South Africa is a signatory to the Convention, the courts will recognize and enforce valid foreign arbitral awards, regardless of the country in which they were made or whether that country recognizes and enforces South African arbitral awards.[112]

8.6 The ICSID Awards

The World Bank created the ICSID Convention to promote sustainable economic growth and eradicate poverty throughout the world. To that end, the bank established a convention for resolving investment disputes between states and nationals of other states.[113] The goal of establishing the ICSID system was to encourage much-needed international investment by offering or providing neutral dispute resolution from both investors, who are (rightly or wrongly) concerned about nationalistic decisions made by local courts and host states who are (rightly or wrongly) concerned about

---

[106] Section 51 of the ACA.

[107] Topher Inc of New York V. Edokpolor (Trading as John Edokpolor & Sons) (1965) 1 ANLR Pg. 307.

[108] Cap F35, LFN 2004.

[109] Section 12 of the FRJE Act renders unenforceable in Nigeria, any judgment or award from jurisdictions that do not recognize judgments of Nigerian courts or awards from arbitrations seated in Nigeria.

[110] Section 16 of the IAA.

[111] Wethmar-Lemmer (2019), p. 382.

[112] Schulze (2000), p. 66.

[113] Amiiche (2017), p. 2.

self-interested actions by foreign investors.[114] According to the ICSID convention, ICSID awards are automatically recognized by all signatory states and are enforced by local laws, including laws governing sovereign immunity.[115]

Nigeria took steps to give effect to its ICSID obligations after signing the ICSID Convention by enacting the International Centre for Settlement of Investment Disputes (Enforcement of Awards) Act on November 29, 1967.[116] The ICSID Act is primarily and specifically intended to provide for the enforcement of an award rendered under the auspices of the ICSID in Nigeria. Nigeria fully complies and adheres to the Washington Convention's obligations.[117]

South Africa is not a party to the ICSID Convention and, as a result, does not recognize or enforce ICSID-awarded arbitral awards.[118] South *Africa* is a jurisdiction opposed to ICSID proceedings, since the matter of *Piero Foresti, Laura de Carli v Republic of South Africa ICSID*,[119] which challenged transformative constitutional and statutory provisions in South African law and resulted in the termination of its European Bilateral Investment Treaties and the promulgation of the Protection of Investment Act 22 of 2015.

References

Abdallah A, Esmail AA (2021) Challenges with recognition and enforcement of arbitral awards in Africa. Available at: https://www.ibanet.org/challenges-with-recognition-enforcement-arbitral-awards-Africa

Abiru MM (2020) Setting aside international arbitral awards in Nigeria: Public policy considerations. https://doi.org/10.2139/ssrn.3715396

Adaralegbe A (2006) Limitation period for the enforcement of arbitral awards in Nigeria. J London Court Int Arbitr 22(4) https://doi.org/10.1093/arbitration/22.4.613

[114] Reed et al. (2004), pp. 4–5.

[115] Amiiche (2017), p. 2.

[116] Cap 19, LFN 2004.

[117] Nwoye (2015), p. 20.

[118] Finizio et al. (2015), p. 2.

[119] ICSID Case No. ARB(AF)/07/01. In this case, a group of European mining investors submitted a request to the International Centre for Settlement of Investment Disputes (ICSID) for international arbitration against the South African government concerning the Italy-South Africa BIT and Belgium and Luxembourg South Africa BIT. The claimants' submissions *in Piero Foresti* included an allegation that they had been denied fair and equitable treatment when required to divest 26 per cent of their investments to historically disadvantaged South Africans following the enactment of the Mineral and Petroleum Resources Development Act, as part of South Africa's Black Economic Empowerment requirements on the issuing of mining rights. The claimants asserted that this threatened their economic interests in South Africa and breached each of the BITs' prohibitions on expropriation. The ICSID issued an arbitral award dismissing the claims against the South African government on a "with prejudice" basis and ordered the claimants to pay part of the South African government's legal fees and costs.

Adedoyin A (2022) Arbitral awards in international commercial arbitration: Appropriateness of review by national courts. NICArb

Adeoye Magbagbeola V. Temitope Sanni (2002) 4 NWLR (Pt 756) 193

Adewale A, Okpara V (2013) Beating the system: Enforcement of arbitral awards against state-owned entities. Available at: https://www.templars-law.com/413-2/

Ahaji Albishir & Sons Ltd V. Bayero University, Kano (1996) LPELR-13928

Aje-Famuyide O, Akano N (2021) Challenges of Nigeria as a preferable seat of international commercial arbitration. Reality Politics 18:24

Akanbi MM (2012) Challenges of arbitration practice under the Nigerian arbitration and conciliation act of 1988: some practical considerations. Int J Arbitr Mediation Dispute Manag 78(4): 325

Akoni O (2022) Limitation period for the enforcement of arbitration awards in Nigeria—City Engineering Nig. Ltd V. Federal Housing Authority. http://www.nigerianlawguru.com/articles/arbitration/LIMITATION

Amiiche OA (2017) Enforcement of International Center for the Settlement of investment dispute (ICSID) awards: the plea of sovereign immunity. Port Harcourt J Bus Law 3(1):2

Amod V. Multilateral Motor Vehicle Accident Fund (1999) 1 SA 319

Arbico Nig. Ltd V. Nigeria Machine Tools Ltd. (2002) 15 NWLR (Pt 1)

Arbitration Act 42 of 1965 and The International Arbitration Act 15 of 2017

Arbitration Act 42 of 1965, Section 31

Arbitration Act 42 of 1965, Section 31, and International Arbitration Act, Section 16(3)

Arbitration Act, Section 33(1)

Arbitration and Conciliation Act, 2nd Schedule

Arbitration and Conciliation Act, Section 51

Arbitration and Conciliation Act, Section 52(2)(b)(ii) and Section 48(c)

Arbitration and Conciliation Act, Section 54(1)

Asouzu AA (2001) International commercial arbitration and African states: practice, participation, and institutional development. Cambridge University Press, Cambridge, p 188

Awoyale OO (2019) A critique of the limitation period for enforcement of arbitral awards in Nigeria. https://phd-dissertations.unizik.edu.ng/repos/81176983800_102282999588.pdf

Ayeni O (2022) Arbitration in Nigeria - A closer look. https://www.alp.company/resources/arbitration/arbitration-nigeria-%E2%80%93-closer-look

Azikiwe U, Onyia F (2019) Global arbitration review— Nigeria. The Middle Eastern and African Arbitration Review. https://globalarbitrationreview.com/review/the-middle-eastern-and-african-arbitration-review/2019/article/nigeria

Baboolal-Frank R (2019) Judicial hostility towards international arbitration disputes in South Africa: case reflections. South Afr Mercantile Law J 31(3):366

Baker Marine Nig. Ltd V. Chevron Nig. Ltd. (2000) 12 NWLR (Pt 681) 404

Balusik D (2019) The know-how to enforcing foreign arbitration awards in South Africa. http://arbitrationblog.kluwerarbitration.com/2019/02/17/the-know-how-to-enforcing-foreign-arbitration-awards-in-south-africa/

Baykitch A, Hui L (2008) Celebrating 50 years of the New York convention. Univ New South Wales Law J 31:364–371

Becker PW (2005) The recognition and enforcement of international commercial arbitration awards in a South African context. Unpublished PhD Dissertation, North-West University

Blackaby N, Partasides C, Redfern A, Hunter M (2009) Redfern and Hunter on international arbitration, 5th edn. Oxford University Press, Oxford, p 513

Brompton Court Body Corporate V. Khumalo (398/2017) (2018) ZASCA 27

Cole RA (1985) The public policy exception to the New York convention on the recognition and enforcement of arbitral awards. Ohio State J Dispute Resolution 1:365–366

Constitution of the Federal Republic of Nigeria (1999) Section 241, as amended

Dale Power Systems Plc V. Witt & Busch Ltd (2001) 8 NWLR (Pt 716) 699

Elias G, Ijaodola L, Oyekan O, Ibekwe V (2022) Challenging and enforcing arbitration awards: Nigeria. https://globalarbitrationreview.com/insight/know-how/challenging-and-enforcing-arbitration-awards/report/nigeria

Eme M (2021) Third-party funding vis-à-vis public policy considerations in arbitral awards enforcement in Nigeria. https://www.mondaq.com/nigeria/trials-appeals-compensation/1142638/third-party-funding-vis-a-vis-public-policy-considerations-in-arbitral-awards-enforcement-in-nigeria

Emelonye UP, Emelonye U (2021) Public policy exception in the enforcement of arbitral awards in Nigeria. Beijing Law Rev 12(1):276

Eskom holdings Ltd V. The Joint Venture of Edison Jehamo (Pty) Ltd and KEC and KEC International Limited and Others (177/2020) (2021) ZASCA 138

Eyongndi DT, Ojuade OO (2019) Applicability of immunity clause to arbitration in Nigeria. Int Rev Law Jurisprudence, Afe Babalola University 1(2):29–37

Federal High Court Civil Procedure Rules, Order 52 Rule 17, and Federal Capital Territory High Court Rules, Order 19 Rule 14

Federal Laws of Nigeria 2004, Cap 19

Federal Laws of Nigeria 2004, Cap F35

Federal Laws of Nigeria 2004, Cap. 522, Cap F35

Finizio S, Morris D, Drage K (2015) Enforcing arbitral awards in Sub-Saharan Africa - Part 2

Fletcher T, De-Waal L (2022) Enforcement of arbitral awards in South Africa: Overview. https://uk.practicallaw.thomsonreuters.com/w-035-3624

FRJE Act, Section 12

Gao Y (2021) A brief analysis of party autonomy in international commercial arbitration. International Conference on Social Science: Public Administration, Law, and International Relations. Atlantis Press:123

Guinness Nig. Plc V. Nibol Properties Ltd (2015) 5 CLRN 65, Triana Ltd V. Universal Trust Bank PLC (2009) 12 NWLR (Pt. 1155) 313

Gutsche Family Investments (Pty) Ltd and Others v Mattia Equity Group (Pty) Ltd and Others (2007) 5 SA 491

Holloway P, October A (2015) Enforcement of arbitral awards in South Africa: Overview. https://content.next.westlaw.com/9-619-5657

ICSID Case No. ARB(AF)/07/01

International Arbitration Act 15 of 2017, Section 16

International Arbitration Act, Section 16

International Centre for Settlement of Investment Disputes (ICSID) Act, Cap 120, Laws of the Federation of Nigeria, 2004, Section 1

IPCO (Nig.) Ltd. V. Nigerian National Petroleum Corporation Ltd. (2014) ECWH 576

Kabo Air Limited V. The O' Corporation Limited (2014) LPELR 23616

Kahn E (1977) Conflict of laws. Ann Survey SA Law:564–570

Khum MK Investments and Bie Joint Venture (Pty) Limited V. Escom Holdings SOC and Another (30169/2018) (2020) ZAGP JHC 7

Kleiman E, Pauly C (2019) Arbitrability and public policy challenges. https://globalarbitrationreview.com/guide/the-guide-challenging-and-enforcing-arbitration-awards/1st-edition/article/arbitrability-and-public-policy-challenges

Kron J, Forshaw S (2020) An arbitrator is allowed to be wrong: Setting aside an award under Section 33(1)(b) of the Arbitration Act 1965. https://www.financialinstitutionslegalsnapshot.com/2020/04/an-arbitrator-is-allowed-to-be-wrong-setting-aside-an-award-under-section-331b-of-the-arbitration-act-1965/

Lafleur J (2021) Africa: Enforcement of foreign arbitral awards. https://www.bowmanslaw.com/insights/litigation-and-arbitration/enforcement-of-foreign-arbitral-awards/

Lane P (2019) The new dawn of international arbitration in South Africa. https://www.39essex.com/the-new-dawn-in-international-arbitration-in-south-africa/

Limak Yatirim Enerji Uretim Isletme Hizmetleri Ve Insaat A. S. & Ors V. Sahelian Energy & Integrated Services Ltd, ICC Case No. 21617/ZF/AYZ
Loukas M (2016) Seat of arbitration and Indian arbitration law. Indian J Arbitr Law 1
Macaulay V. FZB of Austria (1999) 4 NWLR (Pt 600) 599
Manko V, Arends S (2021) Arbitration act: The intersection between remittal and review. https://www.cliffedekkerhofmeyr.com/export/sites/cdh/en/news/publications/2021/Dispute/Downloads/Dispute-Resolution-Alert-4-May-2021.pdf
Metroline (Nig.) Ltd. V. Dikko (2021) 2 NWLR (Pt. 1761) 422, Baker Marine Nigeria Ltd V. Chevron Nigeria Ltd (2003) 13 NWLR (Pt. 997) 276
Mogaila V. Coca-Cola Fortune (Pty) Ltd (2018) 1 SA
Moneke E (2018) Strengthening the legal regime for the recognition and enforcement of arbitral awards in Nigeria. Gravitas Rev Bus Property Law 9(3):3
Mordi M, Sani F, Olutoye O (2022) Enforcement of arbitral awards in Nigeria: Overview. https://uk.practicallaw.thomsonreuters.com/w-034-5855
Mpahlwa M (2017) Challenging an arbitration award: Is it there for the taking? https://www.cliffedekkerhofmeyr.com/en/news/publications/2017/dispute/dispute-resolution-alert-25-october-Challenging-an-arbitration-award-is-it-there-for-the-taking.html
Myathaza V. Johannesburg Metropolitan Bus Services SOC Limited t/a Metrobus and Others (2018) 1 SA 38
New York Convention, Article II (1) and (3)
Nwakoby GC (2010) Arbitration and conciliation act, cap A18 Laws of the Federation of Nigeria 2004—call for amendment. Nnamdi Azikiwe Univ J Int Law Jurisprudence 1:3
Nwakoby GC, Aduaka CE (2015) The recognition and enforcement of international arbitral awards in Nigeria: the issue of time limitation. J Law Policy Globalization 37:123
Nwoye IS (2015) The recognition and enforcement regime for ICSID awards in the United States, China, and Nigeria: An analytical comparison. https://doi.org/10.2139/ssrn.2595833
ObiOkoye OI (2005) Eradicating delay in the administration of justice in African courts: A comparative analysis of South African and Nigerian courts. Unpublished LLM Dissertation, University of Pretoria
Okonkwo V. Okagbue (1994) 9 NWLR (Pt 368) 301
Okoronkwo P (2022) Enforcement of foreign arbitral awards in Nigeria. https://www.hg.org/legal-articles/enforcement-of-foreign-arbitral-awards-in-nigeria-6031
Ostrove M, Carter J, Sanderson B (2021) Awards: Challenges - The guide to challenging and enforcing arbitration awards. The Guide to Challenging and Enforcing Arbitration Awards - Second Edition - Global Arbitration Review
Prescription Act 69 of 1969, Section 11
Rajpal J, Da Costa B, Moti M (2002) Review of an arbitrator's award based on 'gross irregularity' or exceeding of powers. https://www.fasken.com/en/knowledge/2022/02/25-review-of-an-arbitrator-award?utm_source=Mondaq&utm_medium=syndication&utm_campaign=LinkedIn-integration
Reed L, Paulson I, Blackaby N (2004) Recognition, enforcement, and execution of ICSID awards. In: Guide to ICSID Arbitration. Kluwer Law International, Alphen aan den Rijn, pp 4–5
Rhodes-Vivour A (2015) Commercial arbitration law and practice in Nigeria through the cases, 1st edn. Lexis Nexis, p 544
Rhodes-Vivour A (2021) Enforcement of arbitral awards in Nigeria. https://nji.gov.ng/wp-content/uploads/2021/12/ENFORCEMENT-OF-ARBITRAL-AWARDS-BY-MRS-ADEDOYIN-RHODES-VIVOUR-SAN-C.ARB-FINAL.docx
Robertson JB (2011) Public policy as a ground for the refusal to enforce international commercial arbitral awards. Unpublished PhD Thesis, North-West University
Safeez-Naaz S (2019) Getting sorted in Southern Africa: How to enforce foreign arbitral awards. http://arbitrationblog.practicallaw.com/getting-sorted-in-southern-africa-how-to-enforce-foreign-arbitral-awards/
Sammartano MR (2014) International arbitration law and practice. 3rd edn, p. 506

Sasfin (Pty) Ltd V. Beukes [1989] 1 All SA 347 (A)
Schulze H (2000) The recognition and enforcement of foreign arbitral awards in South Africa. Juta's Bus Law 8(2):66
Limitation Laws of Lagos State 2015, Section 52 and 8(1)(d); Limitation Law of the Federal Capital Territory Abuja, Section 7(1)(d); Limitation Law of Benue State 1988, Section 4(1)(c); Limitation Law of Rivers State 1988, Section 34; Limitation Law of Bauchi State 1991, Section 18
Shasore O, Uka OA (2022) International arbitration - Nigeria, trends, and developments. https://practiceguides.chambers.com/practice-guides/international-arbitration-2022/nigeria/trends-and-developments/O11462
Smith J (2021) Enforcement of local and foreign arbitral awards in South Africa. https://www.pinsentmasons.com/out-law/guides/enforcement-of-local-foreign-arbitral-awards-south-africa
SPA Ajibade & Co. (2022) Challenging and enforcing arbitration awards in Nigeria. https://spaajibade.com/challenging-and-enforcing-arbitration-awards-in-nigeria/
State Information Technology Agency SOC Limited (SITA) V. ELCB Information Services (Pty) Ltd and Another (995/16) (2017) ZASCA 120
Stier A (2021) Don't be late—The risk of arbitral awards becoming unenforceable due to limitation periods. https://omnibridgeway.com/insights/blog/blog-posts/blog-details/global/2021/02/24/don-t-be-late-the-risk-of-arbitral-awards-becoming-unenforceable-due-to-limitation-periods
Sundersons Ltd & Anor V. Cruiser Shipping PTE Ltd & Anor (2015) 17 NWLR (Pt 1488) 357
Szászy I (1965) Recognition and enforcement of foreign arbitral awards. Am J Comp Law 14(4): 658
Taylor Woodrow Nig. Ltd V. Suddeutsche Etna-Werk Gmbh (1993) 4 NWLR (Pt 285) 127
Telecordia Technologies Inc. V. Telcom SA Ltd (2007) 5 BCLR 503 (SCA)
Tobi N (1997) Delay in the administration of justice, in Nweze C: essays in honour of Hon. Justice Eugene Ubaezona 21
Topher Inc of New York V. Edokpolor (Trading as John Edokpolor & Sons) (1965) 1 ANLR 307
Tosun HA (2019) Public policy concepts in international arbitration. PhD Dissertation, University of California, Berkeley. https://escholarship.org/uc/item/4xj024n0
Uba UH (2017) Challenges in the recognition and enforcement of foreign arbitral awards in Nigeria. Unpublished LLM thesis, University of Malaya
UNCITRAL Model Law, Articles 35 and 36
Uniform Rules of Court, Rule 6(5)(a)
Wethmar-Lemmer M (2019) The recognition and enforcement of foreign arbitral awards under the international arbitration act 15 of 2017. South African Mercantile Law J 31(3):382
Williams D (2020) Arbitration procedures and practice in South Africa: Overview. https://uk.practicallaw.thomsonreuters.com/4-502-0878

Okadazim Makinde was born in Nigeria. She had her LLB degree. She graduated with her LLM degree posthumously under Prof Baboolal-Frank. She wanted to pursue her doctorate under the same supervisor, though her plans were thwarthed by her untimely demise. She was a dedicated student that dreamt of a family with her husband. She was excited about this book project and would have been excited about the finalisation and her work being showcased.

Professor Rashri Baboolal-Frank joined the Department of Procedural Law in the Faculty of Law at the University of Pretoria as a lecturer in February 2014. Prior to joining the University she practised as an attorney in Cape Town, Western Cape. She practised commercial litigation, criminal law, general litigation and resolution of property disputes. Subsequently to gaining experience as an attorney, she sought to become an advocate. She removed herself as a practising attorney and enrolled as an advocate after completing the necessary pupillage training and required exams. Prof. Baboolal-Frank was promoted to Senior Lecturer in February 2019. Prof. Baboolal-Frank was promoted to Associate Professor in January 2023.

She completed her LLB at the University of KwaZulu Natal. She obtained her Master's degree in Commercial Law (LLM) from the University of Cape Town. She completed her LLD from the University of Pretoria entitled "A Critical Analysis of Tribunals in South Africa to create a harmonised tribunal system". She completed the AFSA postgraduate certificate course in Alternative Dispute Resolution in conjunction with the University of Pretoria *cum laude*. She holds her Master's in Business Administration (MBA) from the University of South Wales in the United Kingdom. Prof. Baboolal-Frank is a leader in her field, as she is a C3 rated scholar by the National Research Foundation due to the plethora of quality scholarship published nationally and internationally. She also holds her BSC (Biomedical) with distinction from the University of South Africa. She has successfully won numerous cases as the leading counsel for litigious cases. She is cited by her peers in academic work. She has been contacted by the media to give her legal opinion. She is often invited as a book reviewer for books that are published in her field and are internationally recognised. She is a peer reviewer for more than ten international and national journals that are recognised, accredited and indexed. She is a registered ADR practitioner on the Commercial and Generalist Panel for Arbitration Foundation of Southern Africa. She is a member of the Chartered Institute of Arbitrators, she is a member of the Asian Institute of Alternative Dispute Resolution, and an Associate Member of the Singapore Institute of Arbitrators.

Chapter 9
Administrative Tribunals in South Africa and ADR

R. Baboolal-Frank

9.1 Introduction

The role and place of tribunals is embedded within section 34 of the Constitution of the Republic of South Africa. People and juristic entities find themselves approaching tribunals as an alternative to the court system, however more appropriately due to the supporting legislation that provides for the avenues of resolution of the dispute. Similarly, to the Australian and United Kingdom tribunal systems that are tiered, specialised and hierarchical. There is a plethora of tribunals in South Africa, that contribute to jurisprudence, administrative justice that ensure that legislation is enforced and implemented in a streamline manner, so that the supportive structure is operating cohesively aligned to the ethos of legislative principles. It must be emphasized that the meaning and place of law in society is entrenched in the relevance to the people, society, and circumstances to hold force and effect. The passing of time has illustrated that tribunals have a firm role in society, but it has not fully adapted to the changing context of society in which we find ourselves in the fourth industrial revolution where technology is taking the lead at the helm.

It is a necessary measure to not do an overhaul of tribunal systems, but to review the systems quarterly for operations and functions and yearly for a complete review of the system's efficiency to make changes for improving efficiency. This will resolve the decrepitude of the tribunals that invariably seep through, due to not adapting and reviewing integration of systems and operations. As discussed by Groves and Weeks that invariably politics play a role in sometimes obliterating the functionality of tribunals due to inappropriate appointment of tribunal members that are not competently trained with adequate knowledge to run a tribunal nor to write

R. Baboolal-Frank (✉)
University of Pretoria, Department of Procedural Law, Faculty of Law, Pretoria, South Africa
e-mail: rashri.baboolal@up.ac.za

R. Baboolal Frank (ed.), *Dispute Resolution within Africa*,
https://doi.org/10.1007/978-3-031-76261-1_9

decisions properly substantiated for disputes before it.[1] These are some of the aspects that have seen the demise of certain tribunals in jurisdictions as well as not receiving adequate funding for operations from government funding.

9.2 Framework of Tribunals in South Africa

There are several tribunals in operation in South Africa. However, it is not quintessential to discuss the different facets of these tribunals when they possess the same framework. It becomes useful to illustrate the framework of the tribunals simply using five tribunals that are popular for the causes of action that find themselves before it. The five popular tribunals are the Rental Housing Tribunal dealing with rental disputes, within the context of the Rental Housing Act[2]; Companies Tribunal consisting of company disputes found within the ambit of the Companies Act,[3] the Competition Tribunal that hear competition disputes as set out in the Competition Act,[4] the Water Tribunal hearing disputes as contained in the Water Act[5] and the National Consumer Tribunal consisting of consumer disputes contained in the Consumer Protection Act[6] and National Credit Act.[7]

The appointment of the tribunal members is through application to the tribunal which also is vetted by the Executive tier of government to ensure transparency, competency and that mutual interests are addressed in a relevant manner. The influence of politics does play a role, which needs to be investigated, if possible, to be curbed, however the converse is that South Africa is not risk adverse to high political dynamics and corruption, so that cleansing of corruption would need to be applied with a top down strategy from government into the variety of facets of lower management to everyone affected in the chain of employment.

The decisions of the tribunal may be reviewed or appealed on limited grounds, usually to another internal forum alternatively if all forums are internally exhausted then the High Court may be approached to consider the respective review or appeal application, as the High Court possesses the inherent jurisdiction to deliberate these matters. Parties are indeed cautioned to pursue unnecessary litigation of decisions to frustrate the other party (winner) and inevitably delay the execution, as the repercussions are punitive cost orders. It is a fine balance to allow parties leeway to litigate and to be used as a tool to frustrate parties into submission.

---

[1] Groves and Weeks (2023), p. 278.

[2] 50 of 1999.

[3] 71 of 2008.

[4] 89 of 1998.

[5] 36 of 1998.

[6] 66 of 2008.

[7] 34 of 2005.

A possible solution to futile applications of review or appeal is perhaps to ensure that the decisions are final without the review or the appeal mechanisms. One could argue that this robust approach is a violation of the principles of natural justice and that errors of decisions would not be able to be revoked. When balancing the scales of justice, there may rather be leeway to manipulate the system than a narrow leeway for denying justice as humans are subject to err and making mistakes. These mistakes must be able to be reconciled through forums of review or appeal. This is not a novel debate and has been engaged for a while.[8]

There is a plethora of tribunals that exist in South Africa, with their own set of rules, geographical location, and members appointed. Each of these different sets of tribunals composes of various causes of actions and disputes such as motor vehicle, medical, specialized investigations, insurance, sectional title disputes to mention a few. Streamlining and harmonizing these tribunals will ensure uniformity, consistency, saving on running costs if it is run from centralized offices instead of dissemination of these expert services and unnecessary travelling costs are incurred. The demand of population density also determines the clusters of tribunals across the nine provinces, constituting of urban and rural areas. If there are no people, then conflict would not arise, similarly in the same vein that the higher the population density then more disputes arise. Due, to the mushrooming of ad hoc tribunals created for a specific purpose, it is difficult to monitor whether the purposes and objectives they were created for whether it was addressed, as sometimes there is an insufficient paper trail or documentation elaborating upon the efficiency and creation of it.[9]

9.3 Reimagining the Paradigm Shift of ADR Within Tribunal Justice

The relationship of the court and tribunals poses a unique relationship. The questions that have been previously discussed by Elliot and Thomas are still relevant 13 years later. The aspect of differentiating courts from tribunals are still pertinent as in some spheres it is described as a "specialized court or a specific type of court". However, in the South African jurisdiction, that is not an issue of differentiation, as there is a clear demarcation between courts and tribunals which differ in substance due to the administrative nature and conduct of the operations of the tribunal. The tiers of enforcement and execution still falls within the courts to enforce unless stated otherwise.

The principle of proportionate dispute resolution[10] is similar to the proportionality principle that the nature of the matter should align to the costs incurred to resolve

[8] Elliott and Thomas (2012), pp. 297–324.

[9] See also Baboolal-Frank (2018). See also Baboolal-Frank (2022).

[10] Elliott and Thomas (2012), p. 299.

the dispute, that invariably the costs and the nature and issues of the dispute should be proportional to each other. In other words that the costs should be fair and reasonable in accessing the complexity of the dispute and overcoming the inevitable barriers in resolution of the dispute. The principle of proportionate dispute resolution aim to address administrative justice[11] in ameliorating access to justice to alternative forums such as enumerated in tribunals.

Tribunals in South Africa are distinct from courts. Courts are relied upon for execution, enforcement and review or appeal mechanisms. There is a level of flexibility more than court process. Judgments or divisions given by tribunal members are rational, reasoned and well thought out. With the passing of time the theory of justice has evolved in enhancing fairness, equality, the principles of natural justice to be heard and given a fair hearing are sacrosanct cornerstones of democracies. The rules of procedure of the tribunals facilitate the process of fairness, equality, a right to a hearing, ventilating, and deliberating all issues to the dispute. Costs saving may not always be undertaken which is dependent on the nature and complexity of the matter and requiring expertise of counsel to litigate before the tribunal.

What is pivotal and essential to reimagining a paradigm shift in a world where technology is leading at the forefront, it is the depth of imagination and creativity. It would mean that to resolve matters expeditiously one could use artificial intelligence to assist parties in utilising alternative dispute resolution mechanisms. There are several alternative dispute resolution mechanisms such as negotiation, mediation, conciliation before activating the tribunal members to hear the matter. Since the Gauteng Division launched court online for the most densely populated province in South Africa, then it follows a natural progression that the exploration of online facilitated forums for the tribunal members to convene a hearing. The notion of reimagination is it empowers one to think innovatively with the aim to create a system that still has a presence, relevance and influence over the people in accessing tribunal systems. With technology leading at the forefront, it becomes the normality to steer ahead of processes through online forums and at the convenience of all parties concerned. The only lag is the current socio-economic and political circumstances. The energy crisis of loadshedding that illustrates an energy grid on a near brink of collapse, it is in the critical stages of barely functioning, municipal strikes that threaten the quintessential services of electricity, sewage and water services. These threats affect the power supply and invariably the respective internet connections throughout South Africa. The reality is that even if one is independent off the energy grid. The signal and strength of internet is affected by the loadshedding schedule, which articulates the time periods that the power off. Irrespective of the positive notions and strides in technology the connection still impacts service providing to all users. In addition to remote and rural areas, the satellite connections are difficult to pick up and hence the strength of internet connections are weak, which makes the notion of having online facilities nearly impossible due to shortcomings of infrastructure barriers.

---

[11] Elliott and Thomas (2012), p. 299.

A recommendation of adapting and altering physical spaces to be more inclusive, welcoming, possess warmth and foster creativity and innovation are splendid ideas to transforming physical spaces of court rooms and tribunals to not being intimidating and isolating for the users.[12] The notion of enhancing the tribunal atmosphere to ensure that it is a place to resolve disputes, and that the users feel a presence of upliftment, inclusivity and want to be there, instead of a place of fear simply creating order and structure to disputes, does not make the environment conducive, as emotionally, one has to convince the users this is a place of use and helpfulness not a place to punish or cause suffering, will also change the mindset of people in which they physical position buildings and spaces and rethink conflict and overcoming it.

The Civil Resolution Tribunal is a good example of innovation and technology with a centralised theme of enhancing access to justice.[13] The artificial intelligence software used to explore solutions and assist aggrieved parties to better understand the law, is a witty and smart idea to alert people to think differently about conflict, and most importantly be part of the problem solving and solution finding called Solution Explorer.[14] The Solution Explorer also uses human experts embedded in guiding the process to obtaining more knowledge about the law, substance, and templates of the matter. If a solution cannot be reached, then the software provides the requisite documents that needs to be filled out to appear before tribunal to deliberate the dispute.[15] The discussion of utilising technology as an enabler and when it disables or isolates the different groups of people, then to bridge that gap using different mediums. Technology should not be the only medium to create solutions nor to prevent the communication between people in ventilating their dispute to finalisation and completion but still harnessing the relationship.

9.4 Court Cases Paving a Dynamic Perspective to Appealing Tribunal Decisions

In this appeal decision to the High Court in *National Credit Regulator v National Consumer Tribunal and Another* (A289/2021)[16] the court had to interpret specific fees incorporated in the agreement to ensure that it was not contrary to the National Credit Act. The court employed the constitutional approach of interpreting legislation within an objective meaning of the text and not the ordinary meaning of not

[12] Gill et al. (2021), p. 63.

[13] Salter (2017), p. 112. See also Alton et al. (2021), pp. 27–54. See also Alton (2019), pp. 151–177.

[14] Salter (2017), p. 125.

[15] Salter (2017), p. 125.

[16] *In Re: National Credit Regulator v National Consumer Tribunal and Another (A288/2021) In Re: Volkswagen Financial Services SA (Pty) Ltd v National Consumer Tribunal and Another (A1042019)* [2023] High Court, Gauteng [Pretoria].

ensuring any absurdity in the interpretation of the text. As a result, that was no contravention of the National Credit Act and the legal fees were allowed.

In the case of *Mdluli v The National Consumer Tribunal and Others* (A195/19) [2022] ZAGPPHC 333 (11 May 2022) it was an appeal to the High Court on two grounds namely costs and interest on the principal amount awarded. The tribunal had held that interest on the capital amount was not proved nor is it automatic following the damages. An appeal court cannot entertain the interest claim since it was not proved by the appellant to the tribunal. The high court dismissed the interest claim. The appeal court disagreed with the court a quo that because the Respondent was absent that legal costs should not follow suit as he did not delay the proceedings. However, even so the money was not refunded until the tribunal had to make that decision to compel the Respondent. The circumstances and nature of the cause of action necessitated that costs be awarded as the Appellant had legal bills to pay which compelled, he should be restituted. The appeal based on legal costs was upheld.

In the case of *Agility Holdings (Pty) Ltd v Company Tribunal and Others* (92,630/2019) [2022] ZAGPPHC dealt with an adverse cost order awarded against the Companies Tribunal, due to the opposition of the costs in the explanatory affidavit. The Companies Tribunal were arguing against a costs order, however, the rules of court provide for costs being granted against the losing party, irrespective, as the Applicant had to incur costs in pursuit of the remedy claimed together with costs to be recovered, as specialist legal counsel had to be employed. This case is important because it illustrates that irrespective of bodies of administration that are fulfilling their legal obligations, that costs order may still be granted against them, as the losing party.

In South Africa courts are still congested despite pilot projects of court online in the Gauteng Division as well as reduction of the trial roll through case management and eradicating settlement of matters to be allocated to the settlement roll. These circumstances are the ideal backdrop for people turning to tribunals for effective justice when warranted. Similarly, Resnick has elucidated the American context that courts are isolating and expensive, class actions suits are not always suitable as it covers the mass objective. Hence, alternative dispute resolution becomes more suitable to deliberate disputes conveniently for parties concerned.[17] It is trite that law is embedded in the socio-political prism of a State.[18]

[17] Resnik (2018), p. 610.

[18] Resnik (2018), p. 675.

9.5 Concluding Considerations in Unchartered Circumstances

There are many leaps and bounds still to be explored and undertaken within a South African context. The use of artificial intelligence has not been scratched beyond the surface nor explored within a dispute resolution setting. Not only for alternative dispute resolution mechanisms but also as an interventionist approach in assisting the parties to navigate the depth of their matters. Technology is not used to replace human intel but to make tribunal systems easier and accessible for everyone irrespective the medium. The aspect of making justice accessible to everyone in any medium is to ensure that the law is for all people and also its users, whether represented or not. Breaking the barriers of rigidity of the law, uncomfortableness of the seat of tribunals and the general emotional discomfort that one experiences, a tumultuous emotional and upheaval of one's world in formalising the solution to disputes. Addressing some of these challenges is to recreate the physical spaces of these tribunals as there are pockets of power that exist with the ethnography of buildings and structures. The power of influence over the atmospheric power balance is an important rhetoric that will reshape the narrative of dispute resolution and the accountability that resides on both parties to deliberate equally before tribunal members.

References

Alton MA (2019) Rethinking fairness in tribunal adjudication to best promote access to justice. Can J Admin Law Practice 32(3):151–177

Alton MA, Furmah S, Seyler K (2021) Adapting the role of tribunal counsel to promote access to justice: how far can we go? Can J Admin Law Practice 34(1):27–54

Baboolal-Frank R (2018) Civil litigation in tribunals in South Africa: creating a unified tribunal system. In: Uzelac A, van Rhee CHR (eds) Transformation of civil justice unity and diversity. Springer, Berlin

Baboolal-Frank R (2022) Appraisal of foreign tribunal systems. Eliva Press, Chisinau

Companies Act 71 of 2008

Competition Act 89 of 1998

Consumer Protection Act 66 of 2008

Elliott M, Thomas R (2012) Tribunal justice and proportionate dispute resolution. Camb Law J 71(2):297–324

Gill N, Allsopp J, Burridge A, Fisher D, Griffiths M, Paszkiewicz N, Potter R (2021) The tribunal atmosphere: on qualitative barriers to access to justice. Geoforum 119:61–71

Groves M, Weeks G (2023) Tribunal justice and politics in Australia: the rise and fall of the administrative appeals tribunal. Aust Law J 97:278

National Credit Act 34 of 2005

National Credit Regulator v National Consumer Tribunal and Another (A288/2021) In Re: Volkswagen Financial Services SA (Pty) Ltd v National Consumer Tribunal and Another (A1042019) [2023] High Court, Gauteng [Pretoria]

Rental Housing Act 50 of 1999

Resnik J (2018) A2J/A2K: access to justice, access to knowledge, and economic inequalities in open courts and arbitrations. North Carolina Law Rev 96:605–675
Salter S (2017) Online dispute resolution and justice system integration: British Columbia's civil resolution tribunal. Windsor Yearb Access Justice 34:112
Water Act 36 of 1998

Professor Rashri Baboolal-Frank joined the Department of Procedural Law in the Faculty of Law at the University of Pretoria as a lecturer in February 2014. Prior to joining the University she practised as an attorney in Cape Town, Western Cape. She practised commercial litigation, criminal law, general litigation and resolution of property disputes. Subsequently to gaining experience as an attorney, she sought to become an advocate. She removed herself as a practising attorney and enrolled as an advocate after completing the necessary pupillage training and required exams. Prof. Baboolal-Frank was promoted to Senior Lecturer in February 2019. Prof. Baboolal-Frank was promoted to Associate Professor in January 2023.

She completed her LLB at the University of KwaZulu Natal. She obtained her Master's degree in Commercial Law (LLM) from the University of Cape Town. She completed her LLD from the University of Pretoria entitled "A Critical Analysis of Tribunals in South Africa to create a harmonised tribunal system". She completed the AFSA postgraduate certificate course in Alternative Dispute Resolution in conjunction with the University of Pretoria *cum laude*. She holds her Master's in Business Administration (MBA) from the University of South Wales in the United Kingdom. Prof. Baboolal-Frank is a leader in her field, as she is a C3 rated scholar by the National Research Foundation due to the plethora of quality scholarship published nationally and internationally. She also holds her BSC (Biomedical) with distinction from the University of South Africa. She has successfully won numerous cases as the leading counsel for litigious cases. She is cited by her peers in academic work. She has been contacted by the media to give her legal opinion. She is often invited as a book reviewer for books that are published in her field and are internationally recognised. She is a peer reviewer for more than ten international and national journals that are recognised, accredited and indexed. She is a registered ADR practitioner on the Commercial and Generalist Panel for Arbitration Foundation of Southern Africa. She is a member of the Chartered Institute of Arbitrators, she is a member of the Asian Institute of Alternative Dispute Resolution, and an Associate Member of the Singapore Institute of Arbitrators.

Chapter 10
The Future of ADR Within the Developing and Expanding BRICS

R. Baboolal-Frank

10.1 Introduction

There are many strengths for the creation of the Shanghai Dispute Resolution Centre to resolve investment state dispute of BRICS. With the imminent expansion of the six member states that have joined motivates more for a centre for resolution. One of the aims of fostering BRICS was to ensure the growing economies by investing in each other State and develop and strengthen currencies. The developed countries already have good infrastructure and stable and political economies. Currently the dispute resolution centre is not active for BRICS disputes, however more measures need to be taken in order to activate it so that the well-respected global centres such as the Permanent Court of Arbitration is not relied upon. The stalling of the commencement of the Centre was due to the covid 19 pandemic that caused a halt to many projects due to the uncertainty of sanctions and travel restrictions. Though with the pandemic behind the global world a new focus to the dispute resolution centre opening and being in operation should be given special attention.

R. Baboolal-Frank (✉)
University of Pretoria, Department of Procedural Law, Faculty of Law, Pretoria, South Africa
e-mail: rashri.baboolal@up.ac.za

R. Baboolal Frank (ed.), *Dispute Resolution within Africa*,
https://doi.org/10.1007/978-3-031-76261-1_10

10.2 BRICS and ADR

The proposition of the dispute resolution centre is not the imposition of fines but merely to ensure resolution of the disputes between the parties.[1] All these countries have signed numerous respective Bilateral Investment Treaties (BITs), Treaties with Investment Provisions (TIPs) and Investment Related Instruments (IRIs).[2] China has signed 145 BITS, 24 TIPs and 21 IRIs.[3] China has accepted the terms of the Investor-State Dispute Settlement, rather than restriction, this has made the difference, in the amount of trade agreements that have been entered into. Although China is pro -arbitration awards and enforcement. Procedures can still be improved relating to the hearing, processes, deliberation of matters the judicial role of the courts and the supervisory role of the awards.[4] China has also initiated the revision of the Arbitration Law to ensure that all the necessary improvements and revisions are made timeously for efficient resolution mechanisms.[5]

When we look at the legal systems of the different countries, it is diverse. Brazil is a Latin American legal system, with Romano-German influence. It is apparent that the Portugal influence of Roman law impacted on Brazilian law.[6] Criminal law in Brazil had influences of German, French and Italian.[7] The legal system of Russia is Roman-Germanic system.[8] The Indian system has common law traits and is based on the English law, which is a past relic of colonialism. India is also incorporating customary law for Hindu and Muslim marriages as a pluralistic regime.[9] The South African system is composed of Roman law, Roman-Dutch and English law constituents as well as a pluralist system of customary law. The People's Republic of China is a socialist state with Chinese principles embedded with the legal system.[10]

It must be emphasised that a simple creation of a forum, is by no means sufficient to create an ideal place suitably formidable for the Investor State Disputes of the BRICS member states. When we analyse for investor state disputes, in particular when arbitration is activated then many considerations have to be taken in account. Some of these aspects is the expert panel to choose suitably qualified and experienced arbitrators, as each country would choose their top five best arbitrators, well trained within the respective jurisdiction to hear arbitration disputes. The language that will be spoken during the arbitration as a consensus from the chosen arbitrators for a dispute, as there should be a universal language for all formalities to avoid any

[1] Fatima (2022), p. 207.
[2] Zihan (2022), p. 162.
[3] Zihan (2022), p. 163.
[4] Gu (2019), p. 171.
[5] Chu and Wang (2022), p. 1.
[6] Vinokurov (2022), p. 38.
[7] Vinokurov (2022), p. 38.
[8] Vinokurov (2022), p. 38.
[9] Vinokurov (2022), p. 39.
[10] Vinokurov (2022), p. 39.

confusion or lag of time lost. Although there are mechanisms such as real time translation using machine automated intelligence that can be employed, various logistics would have to be navigated through. There is a move away from the Western norms of adoption due to the legal matrix of the different systems concerned, perhaps the creation of a system in principle to work for the overall aim and objectives of the parties, affected by the dispute. One of the earlier recommendations was the movement away from awards and sanctions or penalties, there was an imposition that only profits should be gained and that losses must be avoided. However, one must be careful, in an attempt to avoid losses, it is a careful balance to walk to ensure profits only for both parties and that losses be shared equally as context and circumstances must always be studied before decisions and outcomes are reached. Such as the outlook of no penalties or final outcomes may be disparaging in the long term as it does not transfer real power to the institution, and there may be negative inferences drawn from the limitations to outcomes.

The rule of law employed over the dispute is an essential task to be undertaken by the arbitrator/s especially if there is no consensus between the parties. The UNCITRAL model law is a rejected notion as the laws of the Northern global sector, then it begs the questions where does that leave the BRICS States. Each State has the influence of its own model laws, if not adopted the UNCITRAL model law, such as South Africa, when the International Arbitration Act 2017 was adopted it was aligned to the UNCITRAL model law. It becomes a sensitive endeavour to ensure that no State becomes offended due to the renunciation of respective legal frameworks and systems. The promise of more as collaborative initiatives is encouraging to find the common ground of a place to work and overcome any hurdles that prevent foreign direct investment, trading and fostering strong international commercial relations.

The notion of fostering arbitral precedence and jurisprudence is still a contentious area, as parties prefer the flexibility of not being bound by the judgement of another arbitrator. There is criticism of the current bias in certain international organisations that are ultimately briefed by the same clients because the type of decisions that are rendered. The question arises, is that the person that ultimately pays your fees, would warrant favour and over time not becomes an invariable client to ensure the work flows keeps coming to them. Usually, fees are split between the parties, and the forum does the payment to the arbitrator to avoid any undue influence of ethical professionalism. However, the international arbitrator realm is small, and the same people with the same backgrounds keeps being in the same company is unavoidable due to a known lack of diversity in its entirety. Hence, arbiter panels chosen from each country, must have imbibed an ethical and professional standard. Payment is not given by a single country but by the institution. Arbitrators are rotated and no person is allowed to keep serving on the same panel if people have not been adequately rotated. There should also be new appointments made to ensure transparency, versality and accountability by all States to maintain impeccable standards of excellence.

Confidentiality and the publication of the awards means that the parties would have to think about whether they would want it publicised or not. In most instances parties revel in the confidentiality aspects of the arbitration proceedings, as they do not want other States knowing the intricacies of their business dealings with other States. Privacy is generally respected at all costs and kept sacred in the best interests of both the parties concerned.

Other alternative dispute resolution processes such as negotiation, mediation, conciliation should also be utilised, if deals needs to be brokered instead of formal trial proceedings. This ensures that there are various opportunities to resolve a dispute by the forum with shared knowledge, expertise and experience. China and Russia are investing funds into the research and development of automated ADR mechanisms which will also be implemented within the forums as the future forward.

The choice of arbitral seat, should it remain in Shanghai, or should it rotate to different seats of the member states, depending on the dispute, and exercising the principle of convenience for the parties. Virtual hearings may also be conducted, using different computer software and programmes, that is double password encrypted, to ensure against breach of confidentiality and cyber security safety. This also reinforces the notion of investment in cyber malware and software systems.

Harmonising legal and cultural principles from different BRICS states in business relations. One of the markers of good business relationships, is happier people and long lasting relationships. Ultimately, it is important to treat people kindly, with respect and integrity to foster the lasting bonds of trust that will be the dealmakers for many business transactions. Once the reputation of a country loses faith, integrity and standing, it is difficult to turn it around from a toxic business relationship to one that is wholesome, healthy and generates copious amounts of wealth for both States.

It is indeed enthralling about the new six member States part of BRICS for 2024, as there were discussions, about name changes, but for now it will remain the same in navigating the impact that these States will have on investor state relations. Argentina is rich in natural resources. Egypt is a global player in the realm of dispute resolution despite being a place of tourist visits due to the rich history. Ethiopia is the first country within Africa, that gained independence from colonialism, and is known as the liberator. Ethiopia is rich with coffee beans amongst, other natural resources. Iran, Saudi Arabia and the United Arab Emirates known to be rich in oil and creation of opportunity for investment. It has been reported that 22 other States applied to join BRICS as well. It must also be stated that we are currently living in a time of political instability and interstate wars. The Ukraine and Russia conflict, which influenced the global participation of Russia at BRICCS due to the warrant of arrest being issued against President Putin. The Israel war that is weighed heavily against Palestine and decimating women, children and anyone caught in the crossfire with some horrific footage. This is now a time, where States are lobbying along other States for refuge, protection and a voice of reason in the uncertain times that we face as a global citizen. ADR is more important as we navigate through the current crises.

10.3 Conclusion

The potential of the expansion of BRICS to the current six new members in 2024, to the 22 member states in 2025 is endless. There have been mention of digital currency and a BRICS currency and how that would be measured. The one shortcoming of emerging countries is consistency to strive for improvement and expansion with the exception of powerhouses such as Russia, China and UAE, whom have prided themselves by existing in silos of self-sufficiency. The endless free trade agreements within the African continent. The future of BRICS is looking very bright and promising with the current expansions of China across the globe and thriving its economies of scale. South Africa, has a lot to gain traction and improve overall, and the path is paved in stone to complete. At the moment, there is not a plethora of literature on this topic, as the content is still being created in the future, and it is not well documented the BRICS progressions, as there is still not enough that has been equated in action, it is mere discussions at the moment. So we look forward to the word in action for the future, where we can populate the literature as academic scholars of the BRICS future unwinding in motion.

References

Chu B, Wang W (2022) Building an international arbitration hub: China's competitiveness and direction

Fatima N (2022) Future of dispute resolution and investment in BRICS. RBADR 187:207

Gu W (2019) Hybrid dispute resolution beyond the belt and road: toward a new design of Chinese Arb-med (-Arb). Washington Int Law J 29(1):117–171

Vinokurov V (2022) Administrative offense proceedings and pre-trial dispute resolution in the BRICS countries. BRICS Law J 9(1):35–38

Zihan Z (2022) China's stance and participation in the ISDS reform. Foundation Law Int Aff Rev 3(3):162

Professor Rashri Baboolal-Frank joined the Department of Procedural Law in the Faculty of Law at the University of Pretoria as a lecturer in February 2014. Prior to joining the University she practised as an attorney in Cape Town, Western Cape. She practised commercial litigation, criminal law, general litigation and resolution of property disputes. Subsequently to gaining experience as an attorney, she sought to become an advocate. She removed herself as a practising attorney and enrolled as an advocate after completing the necessary pupillage training and required exams. Prof. Baboolal-Frank was promoted to Senior Lecturer in February 2019. Prof. Baboolal-Frank was promoted to Associate Professor in January 2023.

She completed her LLB at the University of KwaZulu Natal. She obtained her Master's degree in Commercial Law (LLM) from the University of Cape Town. She completed her LLD from the University of Pretoria entitled "A Critical Analysis of Tribunals in South Africa to create a harmonised tribunal system". She completed the AFSA postgraduate certificate course in Alternative Dispute Resolution in conjunction with the University of Pretoria *cum laude*. She holds her Master's in Business Administration (MBA) from the University of South Wales in the United Kingdom. Prof. Baboolal-Frank is a leader in her field, as she is a C3 rated scholar by the National Research Foundation due to the plethora of quality scholarship published nationally and internationally. She also holds her BSC (Biomedical) with distinction from the University of South Africa. She has successfully won numerous cases as the leading counsel for litigious cases. She is cited by her peers in academic work. She has been contacted by the media to give her legal opinion. She is often invited as a book reviewer for books that are published in her field and are internationally recognised. She is a peer reviewer for more than ten international and national journals that are recognised, accredited and indexed. She is a registered ADR practitioner on the Commercial and Generalist Panel for Arbitration Foundation of Southern Africa. She is a member of the Chartered Institute of Arbitrators, she is a member of the Asian Institute of Alternative Dispute Resolution, and an Associate Member of the Singapore Institute of Arbitrators.

The manufacturer's authorised representative in the EU is Springer Nature Customer Service Centre GmbH, Europaplatz 3, 69115 Heidelberg, Germany. If you have any concerns regarding our products, please contact ProductSafety@springernature.com

Printed and bound by CPI Group (UK) Ltd, Croydon, CR0 4YY
01/10/2026
02225876-0009